WORLD WAR II

and the

PENNSYLVANIA WILDS

WORLD WAR II

and the

PENNSYLVANIA WILDS

KATHY MYERS

Published by The History Press
An imprint of Arcadia Publishing
Charleston, SC
www.historypress.com

First published 2025

Manufactured in the United States

ISBN 9781467159890

Library of Congress Control Number: 2025934740

In memory of my parents, Winslow and Isabel Williams Smith, part of the Greatest Generation in the Pennsylvania Wilds.

"Honor thy father and thy mother: that thy days may be long upon the land which the Lord thy God giveth thee."
—Exodus 20:12

CONTENTS

PREFACE

Allegheny River at Tionesta, Forest County. *Andrew Myers.*

Lose (or find!) yourself in Pennsylvania Wilds Landscapes and Journeys, covering one of the biggest blocks of green between New York City and Chicago with 2 million acres of breathtakingly beautiful public land…with fifty state game lands, twenty-nine state parks, nine state and national forests and sixteen thousand miles of streams and rivers.[1]

The year 2025 marks the eightieth anniversary of the end of World War II. If you're holding this book in your hands, you are probably considering if it is something you want to read. To help you decide, please know that it is the story about the Pennsylvania Wilds and its Greatest Generation, the people who experienced World War II.

While the Pennsylvania Wilds covers approximately 25 percent of the state's land acreage in north-central Pennsylvania, just 4 percent of the population of the state resides there. If you are planning a visit to its small towns and cities, you will meet locals, many whose families have lived in the

Pennsylvania Wilds for multiple generations.[2] For visitors new to the Wilds, or to those of you who are residents of the Wilds, in this book you will find information about how its small population reacted to the war years both in combat and on the homefront.

ACKNOWLEDGEMENTS

My thanks to the following people and organizations for their assistance with this project:

Andrew Myers, MA, RPA, for the use of his photos;
Elk County Historical Society for the use of its Elliott Company photo;
Pauline Buehler Dunn and Thomas Buehler for photos and recollections about their father, Otto Buehler;
Eberly Family Special Collections Library, Penn State University Libraries, for use of its photos;
Brianna Fleming and the *Tri-County Weekend* for use of its photos on Wilfrid "Bud" Neubert;
Indiana University of Pennsylvania for the use of the 1930 photo, Indiana State Teachers College *Oak Yearbook*;
John Myers, my husband, for his encouragement.

INTRODUCTION

Many years ago, when I studied creative writing in my college prep high school English class in Ridgway, Pennsylvania, my teacher, Mrs. Frances Harvey, advised us to write about things that were familiar to us. Following that advice many years later, I have authored three books for Arcadia Publishing/The History Press about the region that is well known to me, the region I call home, the Pennsylvania Wilds.

As I began research on World War II, the phrase "Greatest Generation" kept coming into my mind. There was only one problem: to me, the term symbolized those who had gone off to physically fight in World War II. However, through my research, I learned that the term is used to define an entire generation, a generation that included my parents.

My parents married in July 1934, during the Great Depression, and my oldest sister was born nine months later in 1935. As the youngest in the family, I was born during the Second World War. As a child, I enjoyed the stories from my older siblings, two sisters and a brother, about the war years. They would tell me about air raid sirens going off at night, when they would pull down special window blinds that blocked out any lights from being seen by planes flying overhead. They also told me that they had a special plan in place should the Germans invade Ridgway—to travel to an outcropping of rocks above town known locally as Mile Rocks, where they planned to hide out in a rock shelter.

It was also during the Second World War that my oldest sister contracted polio, which was still a very real threat in those years. My parents, young as they were, not only faced the challenges brought on by the war—longer work hours for my father in a factory that supplied submarine motors for the navy, food rationing, three children plus a new baby girl—but they also faced a polio quarantine of the whole family for about six weeks. With no assistance from any social services agencies in those years and no pay for my father, they attended to the needs of my sister utilizing the controversial Kenny treatment. She made a recovery due to their dedication.

I grew up with the stories of the Second World War and its impact on people in the Wilds—friends, neighbors and relatives. I have personally known many from the Greatest Generation who went off to fight that war.

In 2025, on the eightieth anniversary of the end of the war, I offer, in the following pages, the story of the Greatest Generation in the Wilds taken from the histories of its twelve and a half counties: Cameron, Clarion, Clearfield, Clinton, Elk, Forest, Jefferson, McKean, Lycoming, Potter, Tioga, Warren and northern Centre.

Part I

THE GREATEST GENERATION

The Greatest Generation Defined

The phrase "Greatest Generation" became familiar to Americans when *NBC News* journalist Tom Brokaw published a best-selling book with that title in 1998.[3] A similar term was used by retired General James A. VanFleet in a speech to Congress in 1953 when he said, "The men of the Eighth Army are a magnificent lot, and I have always said the greatest of Americans we have ever produced."[4]

There are variations in the years counted for those known as the Greatest Generation. One site declares that it is the people born between 1901 and 1924 who came of age during the Great Depression and the 1940s, with many of them fighting in World War II.[5] Another defines the Greatest Generation as those born between the 1900s and the 1920s, with no universal cut-off date, but generally those people born from 1901 to 1927.[6]

Some who study generations have identified the characteristics that define the Greatest Generation: personal responsibility, humility, work ethic, frugality, commitment, integrity and self-sacrifice.[7] World events molded the children of the Greatest Generation—World War I, the Roaring Twenties, Prohibition and the Great Depression. A brief review of those events follows.

WORLD WAR I AND ITS AFTERMATH

In January, 1917, British cryptographers deciphered a telegram from German Foreign Minister Arthur Zimmermann to the German Minister to Mexico, Heinrich von Eckhardt, offering United States territory to Mexico in return for Mexico joining the German cause. This message helped draw the United States into war and thus change the course of history.[8]

A portion of the children who grew up to become known as the Greatest Generation came into a world that was defined by the "War to End All Wars," the First World War. They were the children born between 1901 and 1917, 1917 being the year America entered the war, which ended in 1918.

The annals of history record that the United States was reluctant to become involved in the war, which began in Europe in 1914. Many in this country viewed the conflict as a European affair. In 1916, Woodrow Wilson was reelected to a second term as president because of the slogan, "He kept us out of war."[9] Two events, the Sussex Pledge and the Zimmermann telegram, changed American attitudes.

In 1915, Germany introduced unrestricted submarine warfare when it declared the waters around the British Isles a war zone. The German threat was aimed at merchant ships and included ships from neutral counties entering those waters. The Germans carried out a number of attacks on merchant ships, but on May, 7, 1915, the Germans attacked and sunk the British passenger ship *Lusitania*.

Then President Woodrow Wilson put pressure on the Germans to reign in their navy. The Germans, fearful of antagonizing the United States, agreed to put restrictions on its submarine policy, much to the consternation of its many naval leaders. In fact, the naval commander in chief, Admiral Alfred von Tirpitz, resigned over the issue in March 1916.

On March 24, 1916, shortly after Tirpitz's resignation, a German U-boat operating in the English Channel attacked a French passenger steamer, the *Sussex*. While the ship did not sink, fifty people were killed, with many injured, including Americans. The issue of injured Americans pushed Wilson to give a speech to Congress in which he delivered an ultimatum to the Germans—abandon their warfare against passenger- and freight-carrying vessels or the United States would sever diplomatic relations with the German government. As a result, in May 1916, the Germans signed what was known as the Sussex Pledge, in which they promised to stop the indiscriminate sinking of nonmilitary ships. Further, merchant ships would be searched and sunk only if they were found to be carrying contraband materials. The Germans also pledged that no ship would be sunk before safe passage had been provided for the ship's crew and passengers. The American ambassador to Germany at the time, James Gerard, expressed his skepticism in a letter to the U.S. State Department, believing that the Germans would not uphold their end of the bargain. His skepticism was well placed, as on February 1, 1917, Germany announced that it would resume its submarine warfare.[10]

Local news headlines broadcast the story: "United States May Break with Germany, Critical Situation Develops Out of Warfare on Shipping—The Entire Country on Anxious Seat—Grave and Deliberate Conferences Are Being Held at Capitol."[11]

With the Sussex Pledge broken, the United States cut off diplomatic relations with Germany. In a few short weeks, another sinister action on the part of the Germans, the Zimmermann telegram, ultimately led to the U.S. declaration of war on Germany. On February 24, 1917, the British presented a troubling telegram to the U.S. government. The message was from German Foreign Minister Arthur Zimmermann to Heinrich von Eckhardt, the German minister to Mexico, and was transcribed by cryptographers in Britain:

> *We intend to begin on the first of February unrestricted submarine warfare. We shall endeavor in spite of this to keep the United States of America neutral. In the event of this not succeeding, we make Mexico a proposal of alliance on the following basis: make war together, make peace together, generous financial support and an understanding on our part that Mexico is to reconquer the lost territory of Texas, New Mexico, and Arizona. The settlement in detail is left to you. You will inform the President of the above most secretly as soon as the outbreak of war with the United States of America is certain and add the suggestion that he should, on his own initiative, invite Japan to immediate adherence and at the same time mediate between Japan and ourselves. Please call the President's attention to the fact that the ruthless employment of our submarines now offers the prospect of compelling England in a few months to make peace, signed, Zimmermann.*[12]

With American attitudes growing against the Germans, the press published the news of the telegram on March 1. The news reached the local newspapers on March 2, with one local paper publishing a headline outlining the German actions: "Dastardly German Plot Against United

World War I recruiting poster. *Library of Congress.*

States—Kaiser Seeks Alliance with Japan and Mexico."[13] On April 6, 1917, Congress declared war on Germany and its allies.

It has been recorded that 297,000 Pennsylvanians served in World War I, resulting in 10,278 combat deaths and more than 26,000 wounded; 449 were reported missing in action. Most Pennsylvanians served in France.[14]

It has been suggested that World War I is as distant to today's Americans as the American Civil War, with more emphasis being placed on World War II, the Korean War and the Vietnam War. It is important to review the past to understand what influenced those born in that era.

Following the First World War, the United States was a leading economic power. With many in this country viewing the conflict as a European affair, following its conclusion there was a desire to move the country away from international affairs. The war had been costly to the country. The United States demanded the Allies repay monies that had been loaned to them. The Allies, in turn, placed the blame directly on Germany and devised a system by which the Germans would pay reparations to the Allies, who would then repay the United States.[15]

Prohibition

> *A 57-year-old woman from Edendale, near Philipsburg* [Clearfield County] *holds the jail record for any woman, or man either, in Centre County, having been incarcerated about eight times over the decade preceding her arrest for moonshining. She carried her Bible to the hearing and said "she would take it along with her to jail." She was running her illegal booze joint from an outbuilding because her home had recently burned down.*[16]

Prohibition laws were passed in the United States in the 1800s on both state and national levels. The federal government banned the sale of alcohol to Native Americans in 1822; in 1846, Maine became the first state to establish a prohibition statute; and in 1852, Massachusetts, Rhode Island and Vermont all passed laws banning the sale of liquor. After the Civil War, liquor manufacturing expanded, which resulted in the organization of the Prohibition Party in 1869 and the national Woman's Christian Temperance Union in 1874. From 1880 to 1900, there was a strong prohibition movement in the Midwest, with Kansas, Iowa, North

Dakota and South Dakota adopting prohibition laws. By the early 1900s, states in the South were also adopting prohibition laws.[17]

After the United States entered World War I, the prohibition movement gained momentum. In 1917, Congress passed a law that prohibited the manufacture of all liquors with the exception of beer and wine, with Woodrow Wilson issuing a proclamation reducing the alcoholic content of beer. In 1919, the National Prohibition Act, otherwise known as the Volstead Act, was passed by Congress. The president vetoed it, but was overruled by Congress. The act set 0.5% as the maximum of alcohol allowed in nonintoxicating beverages. The law led to drastic enforcement and strictly regulated the distribution of liquor. In 1920, the Supreme Court, by unanimous decision, sustained the Eighteenth Amendment and the Volstead Act.[18]

It seems almost ironic that a movement, Prohibition, which began during intensive religious revivalism of the 1820s and 1830s was responsible for ushering in "new industries," so to speak—the illegal production and distilling of alcohol with the introduction of bootlegging, speakeasies and distilling operations.

Early bootleggers were involved in smuggling foreign-made commercial liquor into the United States. Their sources came across both the Canadian and Mexican borders, with others utilizing ships of foreign registry along the seacoasts. The Bahamas, Cuba and the islands of Saint-Pierre and Miquelon off the southern coast of Newfoundland were some of the bootleggers' preferred supply sources. A favorite spot for ships to discharge their contraband was at the three-mile limit in the ocean just outside Atlantic City, New Jersey, where the government lacked jurisdiction. The liquor was unloaded into high-speed ships that were built to outrace the U.S. Coast Guard cutters.[19]

Eventually, the Coast Guard began halting and searching ships, which was riskier for the smugglers. That led to changes in the bootlegging industry as they looked for other sources. One source was denatured alcohol, which American industries were permitted to use after it had been mixed with chemicals that left it unfit for drinking. Bootleggers were able to divert millions of gallons for their use where they washed out the chemicals, mixed it with tap water and added a small amount of real liquor for flavor. The final brew was sold to individuals and speakeasies. By the late 1920s, bootleggers had begun making moonshine, liquor from corn.[20]

The Pennsylvania Wilds region had its own experiences with moonshine. In 1920, when state police were looking for stolen vehicles and pulled over

Left: Prohibition disposal, New York City. *Library of Congress.*

Right: Captured rumrunner with onboard contraband. *Wikimedia Commons.*

a truck between Bellefonte and Pleasant Gap at two o'clock in the morning, they found three barrels of whiskey inside onion bags. It was quite a haul—the men, who were from the eastern part of the state, were delivering the barrels for $1,000 each.[21]

Near Philipsburg in Clearfield County, state police raided and arrested the owner of the Central Hotel for having a bottle of moonshine. Near Point Lookout, a ten-gallon still was seized and was taken to the basement of the Centre County Jail in Bellefonte.[22]

In Houtzdale, which is also in Clearfield County, a store on Main Street was raided where three thousand bottles of "Jamaica ginger" were removed, with a homemade still found upstairs. Another store had four thousand bottles and fifty-two cases of the illegal moonshine.

In nearby Clinton County, a man by the name of Prince Farrington was involved in a mammoth moonshine operation near Loganton on his "Florida Fruit Farm."[23] The prince was described as a "superior person." According to the mechanical superintendent of the *Jersey Shore Herald*, Farrington's whiskey was of high quality. And while moonshining was a dangerous business, there were never any tales of bullet-ridden cars in connection with Prince Farrington.[24]

There are also stories from Jersey Shore, Lycoming County, of cars being secretly repaired at night, with one described as a bullet-ridden Hudson with bloodstained cushions. Or there was the custom-made Nash automobiles with two-hundred-gallon tanks slung under their frames, or Reo Speed Wagons used to transport fifty-gallon kegs of whiskey hidden under loads of coal.[25] The local milkmen described how they would pick up orders for whiskey and deliver it along with their regular deliveries for fees ranging from $100 to $2,000. One told of storing moonshine in his barn for weeks.[26]

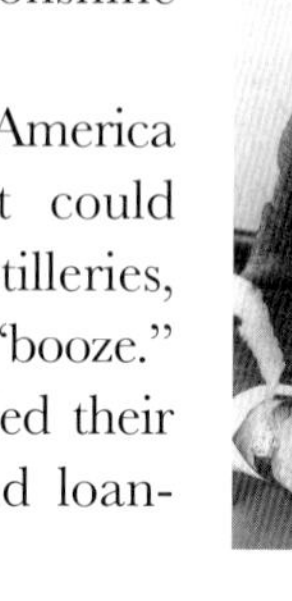
Eliot Ness. *Wikimedia Commons.*

Bootlegging led to organized crime in America with the establishment of gangs that could control the liquor industry from distilleries, breweries, storage and transportation of "booze." Eventually, these organized gangs expanded their activities into gambling, prostitution and loan-sharking, among other illicit activities.[27]

In 1929, the year of the stock market crash, a man was hired to combat the spike in criminal activity, a man who later had a connection to the Pennsylvania Wilds: Eliot Ness.

Hired to head the Prohibition Bureau in Chicago for the U.S. Department of Justice, Ness and his team were dedicated, unbribable agents who became known as the Untouchables. They raided breweries and speakeasies. By 1932, the Untouchables had infiltrated some of these gangs and found enough evidence of income tax evasion by mob boss Al Capone to send him to prison.[28]

Ness was one of the Greatest Generation, having been born in Chicago in 1903. In addition to his crime fighting positions for the Treasury Department and the FBI, he was national head of social protection for all armed services during World War II. In 1948, he was an unsuccessful candidate for mayor of Cleveland, Ohio.[29] He relocated to Coudersport in Potter County, Pennsylvania, in September 1956. While one might assume that this big-city boy came to the Pennsylvania Wilds to live a quiet life away from the criminals and organized crime he fought for so many years, the fact is that he came for a new challenge: to accept a job as president of the Guaranty Paper Company, "a newly formed company that was preparing to market a new process for synthetically watermarking paper."[30] Ness's time in Coudersport was short, as he died of a heart attack on May 16, 1957, at the age of fifty-four, only eight months after he had arrived in town.

Ness's life led to the writing of a book based on his crime fighting experiences, *The Untouchables*, which was published in the fall of 1957 a few months after his death. Much of the actual writing was done by Oscar Fraley, a sportswriter, with Ness and his wife, Betty, along with Walter Taylor, managing editor of the *Potter Enterprise* newspaper in Coudersport, serving as a committee on what to include in the Ness story. The book was not successful; however, Desi Arnaz, television producer and performer, took the story and produced it for television.[31]

Those who knew Ness personally commented that he was nothing like his character portrayed by Robert Stack in the television series. His wife, Betty, remarked, "I like Robert Stack in Eliot's role on television....All but for one thing—Stack is so grim-faced through it all and you know Eliot wasn't like that....I hope to establish that he was just a real good guy who did other things than go around smashing stills and shooting at people. I want people to know that Eliot hated violence. He wouldn't even hunt rabbits because he couldn't stand to see them hurt."[32]

In honor of its famous resident, the town of Coudersport promotes an Eliot Ness Fest. The weekend event celebrates the life and times of Eliot Ness, including his fight against gangster Al Capone. A parade features classic cars and law enforcement vehicles from the Prohibition era. It is followed by an evening of big-band music. A Sunday picnic allows visitors to encounter vintage cars along the streets and mingle with those dressed in Roaring Twenties outfits. Details for the July event can be found at https://www.eliotnessfest.com.

The Roaring Twenties

> *If you can remember the years immediately after the war, you will probably recall that a great deal was said about the wickedness of the flapper in those days. She wore short skirts, she rolled her stockings, she was slangy and irreverent and somewhat skittish, she smoked cigarettes and now and then she took a drink; and all her serious elders predicted a bad end for her.*
>
> *A good many years have passed since then, the post-war flapper is now, in most cases, a mother and Dr. Frances Gaw, Seattle psychologist, declares bluntly that she is doing right well at the job.*
>
> *Dr. Gaw has seen a number of the children of these ex-flappers in Seattle schools, and she says they give every indication of having come from homes that are conducted sanely and intelligently.*
>
> *If you can judge a woman by her children—and it's not a bad gauge—the flapper has turned into a pretty nice sort of person.*[33]

This article appeared in a Warren County newspaper in 1935 under the headline, "The Flapper Evolves." It gives one an idea of how people thought about the Roaring Twenties. But also consider that the flappers were generally not part of the Greatest Generation, the majority having been born before the beginning of the years that marked its rise. In many instances, they were the mothers of the children who became known as that generation. The writer was reassuring his audience that the flappers were very capable parents.

Four young flappers. *Wikimedia Commons.*

The Roaring Twenties were those years that were wedged between World War I and the Great Depression. Much change was taking place in the country. The rise of the flappers may be directly tied to the fact that women gained the right to vote from the Nineteenth Amendment in 1920. A significant number of women went to work during World War I and remained in the workforce after the war.

The country was enjoying an accelerating economy. We take it for granted today, but electricity changed the country forever. By 1927, 63 percent of the households in the United States were using electricity. A newspaper in Jefferson County proclaimed:

> *What a blessing to the world is electricity! And what tremendous hardships the world would suffer, if this modern force were lost to us! Such a suggestion is silly, of course, for the world is not going to do without electricity. In the natural progress of events, we are going to use more and more of this magic 'White Coal', someone has been pleased to call it, and people and whole communities are going to be blessed and benefitted accordingly.*[34]

With electricity, women were introduced to many new items to make housework easier, like the refrigerator, vacuum cleaner and washing machine. A new American pastime was launched as movies became more popular and innovative. There was a rise in the popularity of the radio, and by 1930, 40 percent of homes had radios. The first commercial radio station in the

United States was located not too many miles from the Pennsylvania Wilds, Pittsburgh's KDKA, which started broadcasting in 1920.[35]

Radio in those days was considered an art. In noting a decade of change (1920–30) brought about in the United States on the tenth anniversary of the founding of the Radio Corporation of America, it was said, "The story of a decade in which communication leaped beyond the wildest dreams of years that had gone before is linked with an anniversary which just has been observed. The anniversary marking the passing of ten years since the Radio Corporation of America was founded is significant for the entire field of radio because the corporation has been associated so closely with the great changes which have pushed back world horizons. How great these changes have been it is hard to realize now that radio is accepted casually as one of the biggest of American industries doing a business of more than $600,000,000 a year."[36]

The automobile industry devised mass production practices with a resulting rise in passenger cars. One of the most important consumer products, the Model T, manufactured by Ford Motor Company, sold for $260 in 1924. Generous credit offers increased sales, and what had been considered a luxury soon became a necessity, with one car on the road for every five Americans by 1929. The automobile gave rise to other businesses such as service stations and motels.[37]

In October 1922, the *Clarion Democrat* carried a story about the popularity of automobiles in Brookville, in nearby Jefferson County. It quoted L.A. Leathers, who was selling Chevrolets in that community:

> *Mr. Winters, traveling representative of the Chevrolet Motor Company, has requested me to jot down a few ideas relative to my impressions of my first month's experience as a Chevrolet Dealer. Brookville, PA, is a county seat town of four thousand people and is similar to most towns of its size.*
>
> *Sold 102 Cars in 30 Days. We have been selling one of the popular, low-priced cars for the past twelve years cancelling this contract and taking on the Chevrolet contract on the evening of the first of August, and up to the close of the month we have sold one hundred two Chevrolet cars.*[38]

That would be an amazing record of car sales in Brookville in today's business climate, let alone in 1922. In 1930, the newspaper noted:

> *Forty years ago there wasn't a garage in Clarion: And it took all day to go from here to a neighboring County in a horse and Buggy. But in this year*

> *of 1930 A.D. Clarion has many good garages. It's an astonishing growth for a space of forty years or less—but there's a real reason for that growth.*
>
> *Automobiles have become a necessary part of the busy man's life. They save him years of time, and with the improvement they have undergone in the past years, particularly, they promise to become more and more necessary.*[39]

As the automobile was gaining in popularity and became more affordable because of mass production, a storm on the horizon was fast approaching.

The Great Depression

> *Washington, Nov.—America's insatiable appetite for luxuries and unrestrainable propensity for spending money was held out today as a nearly certain guarantee against a serious business depression, feared in some quarters as a result of the $15,000,000,000 stock market crash.*
>
> *Because Mr. and Mrs. Average Citizens are ready spenders and want several changes of raiment, different type and colored shoes, new automobiles every two or three years, the latest radios and other necessities and luxurious, innumerable, trade should be kept booming, in the opinion of treasury and commerce officials.…America prosperity is not built upon the sale of necessities such as bread and meat and necessary clothing a treasury official said.*
>
> *Prosperity is here because the American people are spending billions of dollars every year for things they do not absolutely need. The sale of necessities may meet business overhead. The sale of luxuries is the gravy that spells the difference between depression, just ordinary times, or prosperity.…Even though the market did crash and billions in profits were wiped out, the people are not going to be satisfied to give up the luxuries to which they are accustomed. They are going to buy and trust to future earnings to pay.*[40]

The above is from a news article that appeared in the *Punxsutawney Spirit* on November 7, 1929, shortly after the stock market crash on October 29, 1929, known in history as Black Tuesday. On that day, some 16 million shares were traded following what had happened on October 24, 1929, when nervous investors began selling overpriced shares with a record 12.9 million shares traded on that day, known as Black Thursday.[41]

Between 1920 and 1929, the total U.S. wealth more than doubled. The stock market, centered at the New York Stock Exchange, was the scene of speculation not just by millionaires but also cooks, janitors and other ordinary people pouring their savings into stocks. The stock market reached its peak in August 1929.[42]

While the market soared, production was in decline and unemployment rose, which resulted in stock prices higher than their actual value. Wages were low and consumer debt was increasing. Due to drought conditions, agriculture was struggling and food prices were falling. Banks had a number of large loans that could not be paid off. By the summer of 1929, with consumer spending slowing, unsold goods piled up.[43]

Following the crash, factories and other businesses slowed production and eliminated workers. For those who were able to hang on to their jobs, wages fell and buying power decreased. Many Americans turned to buying on credit, and foreclosures and repossessions climbed. In spite of assurances from Republican President Herbert Hoover and his administration that the crisis would pass, the economy grew worse over the next three years. By 1930, 4 million Americans were looking for work, and by 1931, 6 million were unemployed. With the country's industrial production dropping by half, bread lines, soup kitchens and homeless people became common. Farmers couldn't afford to harvest their crops, leaving them to rot in the fields. In 1930, severe drought swept over the southern plains in what became known as the Dust Bowl, killing people, livestock and crops.[44]

In Warren, Pennsylvania, on November, 19, 1930, about one year after the crash, the local newspaper ran an article appealing for citizens to come forward to help the unemployed. It reads like a sincere effort by locals to assist with the worsening crisis:

> *Cooperation Needed*
> *I am sorry if my attempt to secure action for the unemployed should have aroused too great a hope in some people of immediate results. I know that the Chamber of Commerce has been doing all it can to place men here and there, who have applied to them, and their list is a long one. The names that we have obtained are for the most part those of married men in Warren who have had work now and then at the factories and who are able-bodied and who have tried their very best to get along so far without public relief. They are not interested in soup kitchens, but are responsible citizens, many of them owning their own homes. They are willing to work, if only for a few days at a low price, so as to tide over the temporary distress....And*

> *more than ever, we would call upon every individual who has any kind of repairing in view to make every effort to start at once. Make your wants known to the Chamber of Commerce. They have a list of men most in need. A few hundred dollars distributed now in wages will be most welcome. Get behind this movement to find work for the unemployed, through individuals, through institutions, and through the local and county officials.*[45]

By 1932, with 15 million people unemployed, Democrat Franklin Roosevelt won victory in the presidential election.

On March 4, 1933, Inauguration Day, the U.S. Treasury didn't have enough money to pay government workers. During this time, Roosevelt famously said, "The only thing we have to fear is fear itself." Following his inauguration, he immediately announced a four-day bank holiday in order for Congress to pass reform legislation to reopen banks that were determined to be sound. During his first one hundred days in office, Roosevelt passed legislation to stabilize industrial and agricultural production and to create jobs and stimulate recovery.[46]

Roosevelt's plan was labeled the New Deal, which included the Works Progress Administration (WPA), a permanent jobs program that employed 8.5 million people from 1935 to 1943.[47] Within the Wilds region, many projects were undertaken under the New Deal.

At the Pennsylvania State University in State College, several campus buildings were constructed during the Depression: the Agricultural Engineering Building, the Burrows Building, Electrical Engineering West, Ferguson Building, Osmond Laboratory, Pattee Library, the Sparks Building and Steidle Building Addition. Overall, twelve buildings were constructed on campus, many of them still in use today. Clarion University, then known as Clarion State Teachers College, benefited from a large construction project, with ten buildings constructed on campus including a dormitory, laundry and new power plant addition. Mansfield University of Pennsylvania, then known as Mansfield State Teachers College, also undertook construction of four buildings on campus, including a home economics building and a gym. Lock Haven University, then known as State Teachers College at Lock Haven, constructed four buildings on campus: the Thomas Field House, the Price Auditorium, Sullivan Hall and a new power plant.[48]

Throughout the small towns in the Wilds, post office construction was a popular project, with new buildings erected in Bellefonte, Clarion, Emporium, Kane, Renovo and St. Marys.[49]

Clearfield and Williamsport constructed armory buildings, while Williamsport built the Bardo Gymnasium, which was part of Williamsport High School between May 1936 and May 1937. A municipal building was constructed in Warren County, a PennDOT facility was erected in Punxsutawney, the Potter County Courthouse in Coudersport was renovated and a Second Ward School was built in Bradford, along with a municipal swimming pool. A sanitary sewer construction project took place in Bellefonte, with waterworks construction projects in Bradford and DuBois.[50]

Outdoor projects were popular, with the Civilian Conservation Corps (CCC) working on the Allegheny National Forest and at the Cook Forest in Cooksburg, where the corps built the Log Cabin Inn Environmental Education Center, originally used as living quarters for the CCC. Parker Dam, near Penfield in Clearfield County, was developed by the CCC from 1933 to 1942.[51]

Numerous projects were undertaken in the Wilds region that provided employment to large numbers of people, with the results of the projects still visible and in use today.

The Depression was a worldwide event, and its hardships led to the rise of extreme political movements around the world, including the ascension of Adolf Hitler.[52]

Civilian Conservation Corps (CCC)

The Civilian Conservation Corps was a work relief program established by executive order on April 5, 1933, that provided millions of young men employment during the Great Depression. It is considered to be one of the most successful of President Franklin Roosevelt's New Deal programs. The work of the CCC included planting trees and constructing trails and shelters.[53] What better area to do that work than in the Pennsylvania Wilds?

Many of the recruits came to the camps hungry and poorly clothed. "They were unmarried, between the ages of 17 and 25. They were called 'boys' but all became men, growing up fast, working hard to put food on the table back home. Food was scarce, bread lines were long, and jobs were few and far between. The boys were hungry and broke, with no hope of finding a job."[54]

Required to enlist for six months, some young men served as long as two years. Issued uniforms, they were given three meals a day and earned thirty

Hicks Run CCC camp, Cameron County, Pennsylvania. *Pennsylvania Department of Conservation and Natural Resources (DCNR).*

dollars per month. Many of the men sent the money home to their families to help offset the effects of the Great Depression.[55] They were able to keep five dollars of their monthly earnings for themselves, which provided for personal supplies and a monthly haircut.[56]

While the army ran the camps, foresters, carpenters and other civilians directed the work. The work of the men included fighting forest fires, planting trees and constructing roads, buildings, picnic areas, swimming areas and campgrounds, with the corps creating many state parks.[57]

Pennsylvania had the second-highest number of camps to California at 151. Due to the forward thinking of Governor Gifford Pinchot, Pennsylvania received so many camps because the commonwealth already had a plan in place for them. A total of 194,500 Pennsylvanians served in the CCC program nationwide. The CCC added greatly to the Pennsylvania Bureau of State Parks.

A breakdown of the camps reveals the extent of the Wilds involvement in the program: Cameron County had six camps; Clarion County, three; Clearfield County, seven; Clinton County, nine; Elk County, six; Forest County, six; Centre County, eight; Jefferson County, two; Lycoming County, eight; McKean County, six; Potter County, eight; Tioga County, five, and Warren County, two.[58]

A Coudersport native, Marie Pryslak, recalled how her late grandfather, George Pryslak, joined the CCC at the age of eighteen, going to Camp Leetonia, one of the five camps in the Tioga State Forest:

> *The thing that comes to mind, of course, is the love I had for my grandfather and the love he expressed of having the honor of serving in the CCC. A lot of the good things in his life were a result of being able to serve there. Looking*

Group of men at Darling Run CCC Camp, Tioga County, Pennsylvania. *Pennsylvania Department of Conservation and Natural Resources (DCNR).*

> *back on the work the CCC boys did and comparing it today is almost impossible. I believe it instilled a work ethic, independence, accountability, pride, friendship and a community. Those boys helped shape the society we live in today.... The skills my grandfather learned in the CCC helped enable his position in the Army. Growing up, I remember how he would talk about the war only if asked, but he bragged about the CCC all the time to anyone who would listen! He was very passionate and appreciative of being able to serve and being a member.*[59]

A few examples of the work done by the CCC Corp in the Wilds include the Lyman Run CCC Camp in Potter County, which later became Lyman Run State Park; Cherry Springs State Park; and Ole Bull State Park, where the corps built picnic pavilions, latrines and a camping area and constructed the original dam in the park's swimming area. At Sizerville State Park near Emporium, in Cameron County, the corps planted several thousand acres of white pines and hemlocks in and around the park. A stone wall that is still standing today was constructed at Hyner View State Park in Clinton County. In 1934, the corps developed S.B. Elliott State Park in Clearfield County, building roads, bridges, cabins, pavilions and trails. The men helped develop two Pennsylvania Grand Canyon State

Parks, Colton Point and Leonard Harrison. The corps developed Black Moshannon State Park in Centre County. At the Cook Forest State Park—which encompasses land in Clarion, Forest and Jefferson Counties—they built single-room log cabins between 1933 and 1935. At Parker Dam State Park in Clearfield County, the Civilian Conservation Corps Interpretive Center, built by the CCC, is still in existence today and open to the public during the summer months.[60]

The program ended on June 30, 1942, due to the outbreak of World War II. Many of the men who worked in the camps reported directly to the armed services. A Pennsylvania CCC historian, John Eastlake, commented, "What they did during World War II is remarkable. Roughly sixty-five percent of the CCC Boys went into the military and helped our country win the war, and forty Medal of Honor recipients are 'Three-C boys.' Many didn't separate their CCC time from their military time, it all meshed together....What the CCC did for conservation was amazing, but when you think about what the boys did to fight for our freedom to go out and enjoy their projects is even more amazing."[61]

Following the ending of the program, some of the camps were later utilized to house conscientious objectors and prisoners of war during World War II.

War Clouds Gathering

On November 10, 1938, on the eve of celebrating the twentieth anniversary of what was then known as Armistice Day (now Veterans Day), the end of World War I, the popular singer Kate Smith sang a new song on her radio show composed by Irving Berlin, "God Bless America." While the song remains a standard to this day, many do not know the words in the introduction that lead up to the more familiar words, "God Bless America, land that I love." But those words were indicative of the coming storm, World War II:

While the storm clouds gather far across the sea,
Let us swear allegiance to a land that's free,
Let us all be grateful for a land so fair,
As we raise our voices in a solemn prayer.

The *Brockway Record*, located in Jefferson County, in the Pennsylvania Wilds, published an interesting article about Irving Berlin's new song:

> *"God Bless America!" Irving Berlin's ringing anthem is sweeping the country.*
>
> *If things go from bad to worse in Europe it is a song that may sweep the world.*
>
> *It is not an anthem of war—but of peace and thanksgiving.*
>
> *Irving Berlin has himself just established a trust fund providing that all royalties from "God Bless America!" be used among the youth of this country for patriotic purposes.*
>
> *The Boy Scouts and the Girl Scouts of America are the first to be selected by the trustees… "God Bless America!" that is what millions in Europe are saying under their breaths.*[62]

Events around the world caused Berlin to resurrect the music and words he first composed during World War I but had not published. And even though Americans were focused on the country's recovery from the Great Depression, the gathering storm was unmistakable.

In the Far East, the United States and Japan had disagreements going back many years. With Japan's naval forces surpassing those of the United States, Congress was prompted to pass the Vinson Navy Bill in January 1934. It was an ambitious build-up of our navy:

> *House Prepares to Pass Vinson Navy Bill*
> *As War Clouds Hover in East*
>
> *Washington, Jan. 30—With preparedness sweeping Congress as war clouds gather in the Far East, the house today prepared to pass the $500,000,000 Vinson bill for a "treaty navy."*
>
> *Democratic leaders asserted there was comparatively little opposition to enactment of the measure which emerged from the House Naval Affairs Committee by unanimous vote.*
>
> *Approval of President Roosevelt to the plan to build the navy to the full strength allowed by the Washington and London treaties—and keep it there—apparently crumpled the opposition of the once strong "little navy bloc."*
>
> *Having given up hope of halting the measure in the House, peace organizations were organizing a national campaign in the hope of killing it in the senate.*

> *The measure was enlarged when the naval affairs committee decided to propose an amendment authorizing a "treaty strength" aviation force in the navy. The program calls for 1,184 planes at a cost of $95,000,000.*
>
> *With passage of the measure, a naval expansion program costing more than $700,000,000 will be under way. The House has already provided funds for work on four cruisers in the regular supply bill, and the $238,000,000 public works grant makes possible building of 32 ships.*
>
> *The Vinson bill authorizes 102 ships to be laid down over a period of five years. Even with this huge building program, the navy will lag behind Great Britain and Japan for several years. Under the treaties all ships could be constructed by December 31, 1936.*[63]

Known as the Vinson-Trammell Bill, it passed the Senate on March 27, 1934. It is considered one of the most significant measures in American naval history. It provided for the replacement of obsolete vessels through new construction and a gradual increase in ships.[64]

The law authorized the construction of 65 destroyers, 30 submarines, 1 aircraft carrier and 1,100 naval airplanes to be started over the next three years and to be completed by 1942. It also approved building 6 cruisers that remained from a 1929 program, 4 in 1935 and 2 in 1936.[65]

At the time this act was passed, Hitler and his Nazi Party had risen to power. Italy was making aggressive overtures toward Ethiopia, and Japan had seized Manchuria and adjoining provinces of China.[66]

Over the next few years, Congress passed other acts expanding the navy: the Naval Act of 1938, known as the second Vinson Act, and the 1940 Two Ocean Navy Act, which increased naval tonnage further and led to an expansion of naval aircraft.

When France fell to Germany and England was under siege in 1940, Roosevelt began to send Great Britain all the support he could short of actual military involvement.[67]

As war clouds continued to gather around the world and German and Italian aggression had already led to war in Europe, President Roosevelt managed to get Congress to agree to a program known as lend-lease in March 1941. As Roosevelt strongly urged, the aid was essential to American defense, as Great Britain was confronted with invasion by the German armies, which had already conquered most of western Europe, along with the rapid conquests of the Japanese armies in China. The act empowered the president on behalf "of any country whose defense the President deemed vital to the defense of the United States, to sell, transfer title to, exchange, lease, lend or otherwise dispose of, to any such government any defense article" not expressly prohibited. The original authorization provided an appropriation of $1.3 million, with repayment to the United States in "in-kind property or any other direct or indirect benefit which the President deems satisfactory."[68]

By the time the war ended in 1945, lend-lease appropriations totaled about $48 billion, with about 70 percent having gone to Great Britain and about 25 percent to the Soviet Union. The United States had received more than $6 billion in reverse lend-lease, mostly from the British and the Commonwealth of Nations.[69]

Part II

WAR DECLARED

Pearl Harbor

Historians record that relations between the United States and Japan were complicated, citing the time in 1853–54 when U.S. Navy Captain Matthew Perry sailed to Japan and negotiated opening Japanese ports for trade. To compete globally, Japan needed resources and therefore needed to engage with the rest of the world.

Over the years, Japan went to war with China and Russia to secure resources. In 1905, when Japan was successful in a war against the Russian navy, the world was shocked, with the United States becoming aware that it needed to prepare for war with Japan. In 1921, the Washington Naval Treaty set out to prevent naval building races between nations and, at the same time, limit Japan to a smaller navy than the United States, which damaged relationships between the two countries. By 1940, Japan had aligned with Germany and Italy. Japan saw the alignment as a way to push back against the United States and hoped that its relationship with Germany and Italy would result in new resources for Japan.

By the summer of 1941, Japan had moved to take Indochina, and its aggression led to major diplomatic negotiations between Japan and the United States. In 1941, the government froze all trade with Japan, cutting the island nation off from much-needed resources such as scrap iron and petroleum.[70]

Burning ships at Pearl Harbor. *Wikimedia Commons.*

Early in the morning of December 7, 1941, while negotiations between American and Japanese diplomats for an enduring peace between the two countries were in progress at Washington, D.C., Japanese submarines and carrier-based planes attacked the U.S. Pacific Fleet, the bulk of it being at Pearl Harbor.

Military and naval airfields near Pearl Harbor were also attacked by Japanese planes, with heavy losses. Eight American battleships and ten other naval vessels were sunk or badly damaged. Almost two hundred American aircraft were destroyed while on the ground, and nearly three thousand naval and military personnel were killed or wounded.[71]

Many may not know that soon after the attack, an investigation was launched by President Franklin Roosevelt to determine if there was negligence by the army and navy that contributed to the success of the Japanese raid on Pearl Harbor. A commission, headed by Justice Owen Roberts of the Supreme Court, made public a report on January 24, 1942, finding Rear Admiral Husband E. Kimmel and Major General Walter Campbell Short guilty of dereliction of duty and errors of judgment. The result of the investigation was that the two men were retired from the service.

But controversy continued, leading to a bipartisan committee opening an investigation on November 15, 1945. During this bipartisan committee's examination of the facts, it was made public for the first time that the United States found success in breaking the highest Japanese secret code before December 7, 1941. The committee rejected allegations made against the Roosevelt government and praised him and other administration leaders for their efforts to avert war. The committee found Japan guilty of an unprovoked act of aggression. While it placed the chief blame for the Pearl Harbor disaster on both Major General Short and Admiral Kimmel, the committee found that they were guilty in errors of judgment and not dereliction of duty. The report censured administration officials for not paying enough attention to intelligence that revealed the Japanese interest in Pearl Harbor. The committee criticized the army and navy for failure to maintain a state of readiness at Pearl Harbor. The Army War Plans Division was blamed for not being aware that Hawaii had not been sufficiently alerted. Due to a recommendation made by the committee, unification of the armed forces of the United States went into effect the following year.[72] By 1947, the Department of Defense, headed by the secretary of defense, had been created.

The *Warren Times Mirror*, in an article published on Monday, December 7, 1942, one year after the infamous attack, expressed its opinion regarding Pearl Harbor:

> *Remember Pearl Harbor!*
> *The government's theme for this anniversary weekend, not unnaturally is "Remember Pearl Harbor." To which Washington publicists add the admonition "Work-Fight-Sacrifice."*
>
> *Our theme for the anniversary also is "Remember Pearl Harbor." But we are free, as government publicists are not, to remember Pearl Harbor from an angle more important than the hate-breeding treachery which the unmoral Japs showed on Dec. 7, 1941.*
>
> *We do not belittle that treachery or its lesson. We learned that day that we were dealing with savages by whom none of the amenities of civilization are accepted. We learned that this war will not be fought under gentlemen's rules; that the law of the jungle is the only law; that gouging, scratching, biting, sadism are the orders of the day.*
>
> *But we learned also that the little brown men of Nippon are no ridiculous little pushovers, inefficient imitators of their betters, ninepins to be bowled over with a single twist.*
>
> *We discovered a year ago today that we had been too complacent about the Japs; that in spite of ample warnings we were fast asleep while the Nipponese prepared to stab us in the back; that our high command had not done its duty for us.*
>
> *Our prime sentiment today should be shame that we permitted the conditions to exist which made the tragedy of Pearl Harbor possible, and resolution that those conditions shall be wiped out immediately.*

Propaganda poster issued by U.S. Office of War Information. *Library of Congress.*

We might also feel a little gratitude toward the Japanese high command for letting us know what we were up against, so that we could get started fact correcting our weaknesses, weeding out the inefficient, tightening our belts for a real war.

If we had learned the lesson of Pearl Harbor when it was thrust into our faces, this viewpoint would be only vicious carping. Unfortunately we did not learn the lesson. Even today, there are too many in high places who refuse to accept its implications, who feel that as soon as we find a few spare moments we can slap the Japs as one would a few mosquitoes.

It is long past time that we waked up.

Let us honor the brave men and women who have died, many unnecessarily, in the struggle thus far. Let us thank God that we escaped paying the full price of our short-sightedness. And then, slightly paraphrasing the immortal words of Abraham Lincoln:

"Let us highly and actively resolve that these dead shall not have died in vain; that this nation, under God, shall have a new birth of more understanding devotion; that we shall work, fight, sacrifice until government of the people, by the people, for the people shall be the privilege of any nation that wants it."[73]

The Wilds was not immune to the casualties suffered at Pearl Harbor. Newspapers reported on deaths, injuries and survivors of that fateful day:

CENTRE, LYCOMING BOYS KILLED IN HAWAII ATTACK
Two Centre County boys, one of who had made his home for years with relatives in Jersey Shore, and another lad from Williamsport, were listed as casualties of the Japanese attack on Hickam Field, Hawaii, where Staff Sergeant Frank J. DePolis of Renovo was killed also. The three youths from neighboring counties whose names appeared on casualty lists announced by the Navy late yesterday are Staff Sergeant William (Billy) O. Brandt, Coburn, Centre County, who was serving his second enlistment in Panama and Hawaii; Private Charles William Narehood, Pine Glen, north of Snow- shoe; and Staff Sergeant Paul B. Free of Williamsport.[74]

FORMER BARNES YOUTH HURT IN HAWAII ACTION
Sheffield, Dec. 20—Word has been received here from St. Marys that a former Barnes youth, Louis J. Brendle, 25, U.S. Navy seaman and son of Mr. and Mrs. George Brendle of St. Marys, was wounded in action during the Japanese attack on Hawaii Sunday, Dec. 7.

The official notice from the Navy Department, received Tuesday by the parents, did not state the nature or extent of the young man's injuries, merely informing that he had been injured.

Seaman Brendle resided with his parents at Barnes prior to joining the Navy several years ago. He enlisted at the Jamestown recruiting station and was a fire controlman, second class.

The news about Brendle is the first received here to date about or from any of the dozen or so local youths known or thought to have been with the armed forces stationed in Hawaii when the infamous attack occurred.[75]

Brookville Man Comes Thru Japanese Attack on Hawaii
DuBois, Dec. 17—Pete Grady, a well-known resident of Brookville, came safely through the Jap attack on Hawaii, according to a cablegram received Wednesday morning by DuBois friends.

Grady, while a resident of Brookville, received his initial air training at the DuBois airfield and entered the American air forces at Chanute Field, Ill.[76]

While people on the U.S. mainland didn't experience the heinous attack on Pearl Harbor, it inspired young Americans to take action. Washington reported that a total of 11,303 men enlisted at regular navy recruiting stations during the first eight days following the Japanese attack on Hawaii.[77]

War with Germany and Italy Declared by Congress, December 11, 1941

When war broke out in Europe in 1939, people in the States were not particularly concerned, considering it a European matter, and the United States was still suffering through the effects of the Great Depression. However, President Franklin Roosevelt was monitoring events around the world and saw German, Italian and Japanese aggression as a real threat. In 1941, Roosevelt convinced Congress to agree to a lend-lease agreement between the United States and the British. The act was passed on March 11, 1941. The United States loaned the island nation fifty old destroyers in return for the lease of bases in the Western Hemisphere. This was at a time when German U-boats were sinking American merchant ships carrying war supplies to England.[78]

What many today reading the account of our involvement in World War II may not realize is that prior to 1940, the United States did not have a peacetime draft. Congress, acting to build U.S. forces, passed a law in September 1940 ushering in the nation's first peacetime draft. In

Pennsylvania, Governor James organized the county and state boards necessary to enroll eligible men into the draft process. In February 1941, Pennsylvania opened the New Cumberland Reception Center outside of Harrisburg. By the end of the war, 844,900 males in Pennsylvania had gone into the armed services via the draft, with more than 500,000 of them having been inducted at the New Cumberland facility. February 1941 also saw the federal government induct Pennsylvania National Guard units into national service. The 28th Infantry Division, with more than 17,000 soldiers, assembled at Indiantown Gap Military Reservation. Taking part in military maneuvers at various locations in the United States, the unit was eventually sent to England in the fall of 1943.[79]

Part III

THE WILDS STEPS UP TO SUPPORT THE WAR EFFORT

Recruitment

The attack on Pearl Harbor was a rallying cry for many young men, who voluntarily enlisted. The *Express*, the local Lock Haven newspaper, printed this on December 12, 1941, just days following the attack:

> *Big Recruiting Boom Here*
> *And All Over the Nation*
>
> *Herbert A. Fisher of 218½ Bellefonte Avenue, was one of five men who enlisted at the U.S. Army recruiting station in Williamsport yesterday as Sergeant Ralph B. Wiggins, in charge, made plans to establish substations in his territory, including one at Lock Haven to take care of an expected rush for enlistments in view of the war with Germany, Italy and Japan.*
>
> *The Lock Haven office, in the basement of the Post Office building, will be open from 9 to 4. It will be in charge of Miss Christine Caprio, one of the WPA clerical workers who will be in charge of the substations, Milton, Lewisburg, Muncy, Wellsboro and Coudersport....Enlistments Multiply, Washington: Dog-tired recruiting officers pointed happily to jam-packed stations today and reported applications up ten to twenty-fold, enlistments at least doubled.*
>
> *Men who remember Pearl Harbor and want to fight about it have been waiting in line for hours at army, navy and marine recruiting headquarters throughout the country—and they've almost worn the recruiting officers down.*

It has gotten so in many places that when the offices shut down after a 16- to-18-hour stretch, volunteers not yet reached are demanding cards entitling them to the top places in line the next day.[80]

By December 19, 1941, the government had announced that married men could now enroll under certain circumstances:

Married Men May Enlist
Voluntary enlistments are now being made in the Army of the United States. Enlistments in the Regular Army has been discontinued. Enlistments are for the duration of the war and for six (6) months thereafter. This announcement was made Dec. 15, by Major General Henry C. Pratt, commanding general of the Third Corps Area headquarters in Baltimore, Maryland.

Married men whose dependents have sufficient means of support and who sign a statement to that effect may now voluntarily enlist in the Army of the United States.

It was also announced that civilians who have received their army physical examinations preliminary to induction under the Selective Service act may be enlisted in the Army of the United States on the condition that the applicant's Selective Service board is notified by the Recruiting serviced without delay immediately after enlistment. Prior to this ruling, citizens in this category were not allowed to voluntarily enlist.[81]

In Jefferson County on January 22, 1942, the *Jeffersonian-Democrat* reported an increase in enrollments at DuBois, located in Clearfield County, and also noted the names of Jefferson County men who enlisted:

Navy Enrollments at Dubois Increase
The Navy Recruiting Sub-station at DuBois this week reported that the number of recent enlistments bids fair to break all enlistment records there. Seventy-six men have applied for enlistment since January 1. Forty-four of these were accepted after a preliminary examination. Of the forty-four three were temporarily accepted making thirty-one applicants accepted.

Among those who have enlisted since January 9 are the following men from Jefferson County:: James E. Holt, R.D. 1, Brockway; George J. Costion, 1049 Fourth Avenue, Brockway; John M. DeSantis, 1973 Second Avenue, Brockway; Wallace G. Clark, Brockway; David R. Anderson 550 South Street, Brockway; Donald F. Shirey, Punxsutawney; William D. Welsh, George H. Welsh, Big Run; Lewis C. Murray, R.D. 1, Brookville.[82]

As recruitment was high and the draft instituted, not everyone was "on board" with going to war. And while World War II has been described as "good vs. evil," there were those whose religious views prohibited them from fighting. Pacifists who were known as conscientious objectors (COs) were required to report to their local draft boards in spite of their religious beliefs and were presented with three options: joining the armed forces in noncombatant roles such as medic or chaplain; joining the Civilian Public Service; or, for those who refused those options, imprisonment. About twenty-five thousand men joined the armed forces in noncombatant roles, with about twelve thousand joining the Civilian Public Service. About six thousand refused to participate and were imprisoned.[83]

The Civilian Public Service was designed to carry on work of national importance under civilian direction. Within the Wilds, members of the Civilian Public Service worked as ward attendants at Warren State Hospital. Others worked at two former Civilian Conservation Corps Camps—Red Bridge near Kane and Duhring near Marienville.

At Warren State Hospital, the men worked varying shifts, some days 7:00 a.m. to 7:00 p.m. while other days were 7:00 a.m. to 5:30 p.m. They were paid fifteen dollars per month according to Selective Service regulations and given room and board. The men received their uniforms. At the CCC camps in the Allegheny National Forest, the projects were designated of national importance. They worked a forty-hour week with no pay and were required to furnish their own equipment and board. They were sponsored by church groups known as peace churches that provided food and equipment.[84]

One conscientious objector, Robert L. Coolidge, who was a native of Wellsboro in Tioga County, gave a statement to the local newspaper hoping to clarify misconceptions about his beliefs and his service to the country. It reads in part:

> *An Explanation*
> *While home on furlough from Civilian Public Service Camp No. 29 about six weeks ago, I found considerable misunderstanding among people from various parts of Tioga county as to where I am and what I am doing…It is my conviction that there can be no just war either aggressive or in resistance to aggression. For nothing can be accomplished by war that could not be better attained by other methods. It is my firm belief that war invariably does more harm than good. It is therefore not ethical. And being unethical, it is unchristian. Indeed Jesus did present a law of love and indicated that evil should be withstood by adherence to that law rather than by violence.*

I am therefore a conscientious objector to all participation in war. I must in conscience refuse to bear arms or participate in any activity for the purpose of helping in a war effort. I recognize that the endeavors most essential to the welfare of mankind in time of peace are in time of war also essential to the war effort….I am now a member of the Civilian Public Service Unit at Springfield State Hospital, Sykesville, Maryland. Civilian Public Service is a program of work of national importance under civilian direction designated by the president as alternative service for religious objectors to war. The objectors drafted and assigned to CPS are not paid. In fact the government does not feed or clothe them. The government provides supervision of the project work and the use of abandoned CCC camps and equipment once used by CCC men such as barracks with cots and a large share of the bedding, cooking equipment, etc. Aside from the work project the camps are administered by non-governmental agencies….Men in these camps may volunteer for service in the following CPS projects: Agricultural research; work on dairy farms; butterfat testing for Dairy Herd Improvement Associations; hookworm eradication; public health service in Puerto Rico; guinea pig service in medical research; work as attendants in mental hospitals, general hospitals, and reform schools; coast and geodetic survey; parachute jumping to fight forest fires. In none of these services do the men receive more than meager expenses.[85]

In August 1942, Harrisburg notified the local Selective Service board of occupations that were essential to the war effort:

DRAFT BOARDS NOTIFIED OF 112 CRITICAL OCCUPATIONS
Harrisburg, Aug. 22—Pennsylvania's 422 local selective service boards were notified today of 112 "critical occupations" that have been certified by the War Manpower Commission as essential to the war effort.

Col. Benjamin F. Evans, acting state draft director, said the list was limited to occupations requiring at least six months training.

The list includes accountants, chemists, boilermakers, derrickmen, coke burners, drillers, electricians, various type of engineers, geologists, machinists, tool dressers, yardmasters, foreman, riggers, metallurgists and welders.[86]

Women's services were also in demand in many instances to relieve men of their duties to go off and fight in the war. On May 15, 1942, the Women's Army Auxiliary Corps (WAAC) was formed to give women who served in the army similar rights and benefits as male service members. While the

Recruitment poster. *Library of Congress.*

law represented significant progress for women, it was lacking military status. Women did not receive overseas pay and were ineligible for government life insurance. If women died in the line of duty, there was no death benefit due their family. On July 1, 1943, remedial legislation was signed into law granting women all the rank, privileges and benefits of men, and the WAAC was renamed Women's Army Corps (WAC), part of the U.S. Army.[87]

Four main fields of work were available for women: clerical, culinary, medical and transportation. While women were banned from combat and combat zones, forty-five Pennsylvania women were recorded as dying in the line of duty. One such woman was Charlotte R. Lucas, a native of Clinton County in the Pennsylvania Wilds.

Charlotte was born on December 4, 1923, to Claude and Hannah Emenhiser Lucas, one of eight siblings. Her father worked in farming, and her mother was a homemaker. In May 1944, Lucas enlisted in the Women's Army Corps at Harrisburg. Reporting to Fort Oglethorpe, Georgia, in June, she was assigned to the 3rd Women's Army Corps Company, stationed at the Hampton Roads Port of Embarkation in Virginia.

The company's members organized the shipment of soldiers, nurses and supplies overseas and organized arrivals and departures, travel and housing. Some women worked as secretaries, stenographers, vehicle mechanics, technicians, interpreters, dispatchers and inspectors. In November 1945, 127,000 people left the port, and more than 152,000 tons of cargo were sent out.

Lucas was stationed at Camp Patrick Henry, Newport News, Virginia, which was a staging area for embarkation from the Hampton Roads port. The camp was also used for more than five thousand German and Italian prisoners of war from 1944 to 1945.

Unfortunately for Lucas, she did not live to see the end of the war and peace restored in the world. On November 9, 1945, at Station Hospital, Camp Patrick Henry, she was run over by a truck and died from her injuries.

Lucas is memorialized on the Clinton County Honor Roll plaque of 190 World War II fallen at Riverbank Park, Lock Haven.[88]

There was also a severe nursing shortage:

> *NURSES ARE NEEDED FOR SERVICE WITH THE ARMY AND NAVY*
> *Retired and Inactive Nurses Can Replace Those Now Volunteering for Military Service*
>
> *On July 1, 1942, in the beautiful garden of the American Red Cross Headquarters in Washington, D.C., six Army Nurses were decorated for outstanding service at Bataan and Corregidor.*
>
> *Mrs. Franklin D. Roosevelt in addressing these nurses stated she had four sons in the service and said, "I ask for my boys what every mother has a right to ask—that they be given full and adequate nursing care should the time come when they need it. Only nurses who have volunteered can give it. You must not forget that nurses have it in their power to bring back some who otherwise surely will not return."*[89]

Ann Marie Frederico was born in Ridgway, Elk County, in the Pennsylvania Wilds on July 26, 1922. She was the daughter of Italian immigrants Sam and Angeline DiVittorio Frederico. It was a close-knit family, Anne being one of eight children, with two brothers and five sisters.

A graduate of Ridgway High School, Anne entered the Reading Hospital School of Nursing on September 9, 1941. She enrolled in the Army Nursing Corp in July 1943, and upon her graduation on September 8, 1944, she entered active service as a second lieutenant at Fort George Meade, Maryland. She was first assigned to the *General G.O. Squirer*, a transport ship working in Europe.

Anne was later assigned to the *Marigold*, an army hospital ship serving in both Europe and the Pacific. It was on the hospital ship where she met her future husband, Albert Hargrave, a native of New Jersey.

The U.S. Army Hospital Ship *Marigold* was built in 1920 as a passenger/cargo ship known as SS *Old North State*. In 1922,

Opposite: "Wanted: More Navy Nurses." *Library of Congress.*

Left: USHS *Marigold* at Tacoma, Washington, following commission as hospital army ship. *Wikimedia Commons.*

the ship was acquired by United States Line, and the name was changed to SS *President VanBuren*. The ship was transferred to the Dollar Steamship Company in 1924, retaining its name. By 1936, the ship was out of service in San Francisco. Returned to service in 1940 and operated by American President Lines, the ship was known as *President Fillmore*. It was requisitioned by the War Shipping Administration in 1942 and during that time was utilized for troop carrying primarily to Alaska.

In October, 1943, the ship was purchased by the War Shipping Agency and converted to a hospital ship at the Seattle-Tacoma Shipyard, where it was renamed the U.S. Army Hospital Ship *Marigold*.[90] The ship's first service in 1944 was in the Mediterranean to care for wounded soldiers from the European front. Eventually, the ship was transferred to the Pacific, where it entered ports in Manila, Milne Bay, Luzon, Biak, Hollandia and Leyte. In the summer of 1945, the *Marigold* was the first Allied ship to arrive in Japan and was present when the Japanese signed the Instrument of Surrender on board the battleship USS *Missouri*. Following the surrender, the ship spent three weeks caring for liberated prisoners of war, not only American troops but also Australian, British, Canadian, Dutch, Greek, Chinese and Japanese patients. Eventually, civilians also received care in space that had been previously utilized for troops.

Anne was discharged from the army June 26, 1946. She and her husband, Al, eventually returned to her hometown of Ridgway, where they raised their family of three children. Anne was an employee of Elk County General Hospital for many years before she and her husband retired to North Carolina and New Jersey.

Anne's wartime experiences contributed to the person who was fondly remembered in her obituary in 2018—a woman grounded in her Catholic faith, someone who welcomed Fresh Air kids from the city into her home, along with nieces, nephews and cousins for the summer. She hosted foreign exchange students and nurses and doctors new to town. She helped to care for many people in the community. She was a tireless worker, quick to smile. In her obituary, readers were encouraged to "Say a prayer to St. Theresa, Anne's patron saint, give blood to the Red Cross, be generous to others, and do a good deed in her memory."[91]

Industry

"The only thing we have to fear is fear itself." FDR repeated his famous remark made in 1933 during the Great Depression on May 27, 1941, when he announced a "state of unlimited national emergency in response to Nazi Germany's threats of world domination."[92] During his radio broadcast, he laid out his administration's policy concerning the war in Europe. Promising the protection of shipping in the Atlantic and continued humanitarian and military aid to Britain, he also established a civilian defense. He urged organized labor to resist strikes in war production industries and condemned war profiteering.[93]

In Pennsylvania, Governor James pledged that Pennsylvania would become an "arsenal of America." The Commerce Department estimated that by July 1941, 20.73 percent of annual industrial production of the state was for defense. With orders pouring in for steel, munitions and equipment, only seventeen counties that were without industry were without sizeable orders.[94]

The following are examples of just some of the unique industries found in the Pennsylvania Wilds during World War II. Reading through these examples, it becomes clear that massive numbers of workers were required to carry out manufacturing. The small towns in the Wilds were flooded with workers being bused into the communities to fill vacancies that were created when others went off to war, as well as due to increased production to fuel the war.

Sylvania Electric Products, Emporium, Pennsylvania

Emporium, county seat of Cameron County, had a population of 3,775 in 1940. With the creation of Sylvania Electric Products, it manufactured needed components for World War II, and during those years, the population of Emporium swelled with the number of women who came to work there, becoming known as "Girl's Town."

Sylvania Electric Products had its beginning in 1907, when a new factory was built in Emporium to produce carbon-filament lamps. At that time, it was known as the Novelty Incandescent Lamp Company with miniature specialty and decorative lamps being produced by twelve women and two men.[95]

The company ownership changed over the years, including General Motors and General Electric. The Depression following World War I led to a decision to close Novelty. Three local businessmen—Bernard Erskine, Joseph Wortman and Guy Felt—made the decision to take a risk to purchase the company from General Electric for $350,000. Production was moved to St. Marys, and the general offices were headquartered in Emporium.

A new craze was sweeping the nation in the form of radio, and the core of a radio was a tube that required the same manufacturing process as an incandescent lamp. A new company was formed, and Sylvania Products Company began producing a new type of radio tube in 1924. In 1929, a new factory was built in Emporium, and several new products were patented.[96]

Sylvania historic sign, Emporium, Pennsylvania. *PHMC.*

In 1940, the National Defense Research Committee began a top-secret project to develop a special fuse resulting in what was known as a proximity fuse. These fuses did not depend on time-to-target calculations or physical contact with a target. This new fuse sent radio waves measuring the time it would take for the waves to bounce back, allowing it to detonate a set distance from an object.

The National Defense Research Committee contracted with several companies in addition to Sylvania. But within twenty-nine days of contract in the spring of 1942, the first fuses were shipped from Sylvania. A few months after Pearl Harbor, the company switched almost completely to war production.

During this time, Emporium gained the reputation as "Girl's Town" when *Collier's* magazine ran an article about it on November 21, 1942. As young women from surrounding farms gravitated to Emporium for work, the magazine noted, "Boom towns are common place phenomena in every war, but WWII has made quiet little Emporium, deep in the Bucktail Mountains of Pennsylvania, the nation's first girl's town."[97]

A newspaper in another small town in the Wilds took a different point of view on the magazine article:

> *Reading of the current issue of* Collier's *magazine in which Emporium is described vividly and interestingly as a "Girl's Town" gives the feeling that the community can well be the forerunner of a great many other small communities in all parts of the nation.... When a community...sends as many hundreds of men into the armed forces as we have done, the work must either be done by women or left undone. The national war effort from the employment standpoint has been ill planned. Certain cities and towns have been given munitions plants, warehouses, airplane factories and other government plants and the wages paid in these factories have been large enough to attract men from employment in other and less fortunate communities. Men from surrounding communities leave their relatively low-paid jobs and rush to the big government plants. It is as inevitable as water seeking its own level. This phase of the war cannot be changed at this time.... Women must do the work or the plants must close their doors.*[98]

The *Collier's* article added that men didn't have the patience or skill with their fingers that the work required. It would appear that there is some credibility to the work requiring the patience and skill of women, based on Sylvania's founding history in 1907, when the company was already employing more women than men.

The secret product that was manufactured in Emporium was an important technological innovation in World War II and is credited for turning the tide at the Battle of the Bulge and the defeat of the Japanese air force and navy. On November 5, 1942, Sylvania received the Army-Navy "Excellence in Production" or (E) Award, recognizing its outstanding contribution to the war. Only 5 percent of more than eighty-five thousand companies producing products for the war effort received this award.[99]

Reporting on the Pennsylvania Historic and Museum Commission's Historical Marker Program (PHMC) and her representation at the dedication of the Sylvania marker in 2021, Andrea L. MacDonald, daughter of one of those Sylvania girls, said, "I have been honored to represent the PHMC at a few historical marker dedications over the years, but until this year, there has not been a marker connected to *my* story until the dedication of Sylvania Electric Products in Emporium, Cameron County. At the dedication ceremony for the Sylvania marker, I learned the military and global significance of this industry, which was not based in Philadelphia or Pittsburgh, but rather grew its roots in the woods of Pennsylvania"[100]—in the heart of the Pennsylvania Wilds.

Elliott Company, Ridgway, Pennsylvania

In the 1940 census, Ridgway Borough's population was reported as 6,253, with Ridgway Township adding another 2,375 people. Manufacturing was a big part of the history of the county seat of Elk County. One of the biggest employers of the day was the Elliott Company, which was in existence until 1962, when it was closed and the buildings sold. Those manufacturing buildings are still in existence today.

The Ridgway works of the Elliott Company came into being in 1927. Previously known as the Ridgway Manufacturing Company, it was located in downtown Ridgway along Main Street in 1892.

It had its start, in part, in 1884 when J.H. McEwen organized a limited partnership and established a general machine shop, foundry and boiler shop. McEwen constructed a new plant in 1892 where he specialized in engine building. Two years later, he entered the electrical field. Soon after, he moved on, and local capitalists bought the company.

Specializing in the manufacture of crank steam engines and D.C. generators, the company's name was changed to the Ridgway Dynamo and Engine Company. From 1897 until the early 1920s, the company enjoyed excellent business earnings; however, little of the earnings were put back into the business, and in the 1920s, the company was having financial difficulties. In 1927, the Ridgway Dynamo and Engine Company was purchased by the Elliott Company of Jeanette, Pennsylvania. The new owners produced various products relating to the electrical field, generators and motors and added new additions to its products.

By the time the United States entered World War II, the Ridgway division was supplying electrical propelling machinery for U.S. Navy submarines. In those war years, the company employed more than 1,200 workers, many of them commuting from outside of Ridgway to fill the jobs. In 1942 and

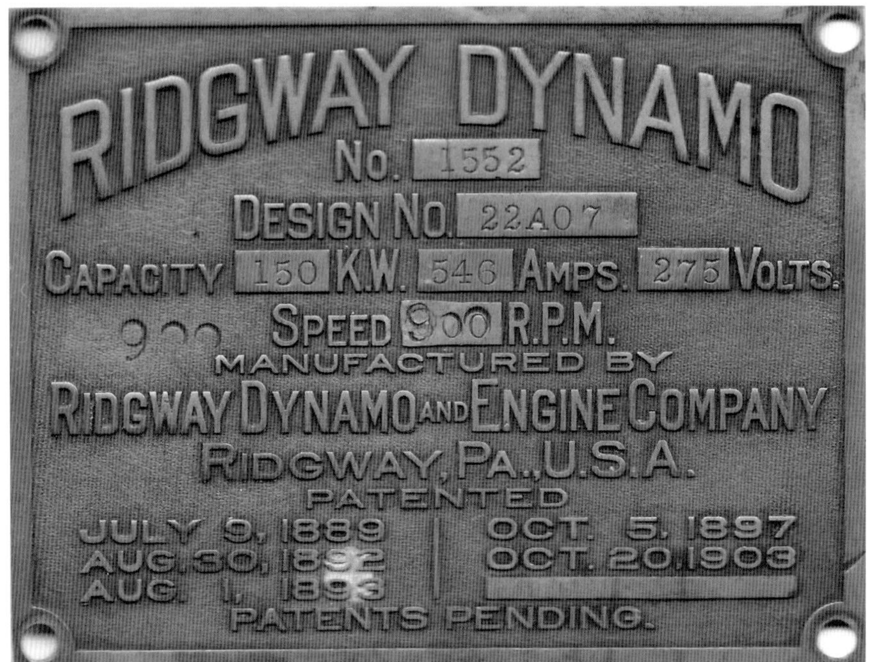

Ridgway Dynamo plaque. *Kathy Myers.*

Elliott Company complex. *Elk County Historical Society.*

1943, the Elliott Company was awarded the Army-Navy "E" Award for its contributions to the war effort.[101]

On March 30, 1943, Rear Admiral W.C. Watts, USN (Retired), speaking to the employees of the Elliott Company at an award ceremony to present the Army-Navy Production Award to the Ridgway Plant, noted, "Steady, routine, day-in and day-out endeavor is required. That, with confidence in our leaders, loyalty to our immediate superiors and trust in God, can alone bring us the earliest victory that is possible and save the lives of thousands of our brave fighting men."[102]

Lieutenant Colonel Thomas Eddy, executive officer of the Pittsburgh Ordnance District, told the employees that the armed forces appreciated what the Elliott Company employees had done and asked for more. "It may be within your power to save many lives by helping to bring this war to an end sooner—either by one week, one hour or even one minute."[103]

Howard Hubbard, president of the Elliott Company, said that the workers at Ridgway were partners with America's fighting forces, playing a real part in speeding final victory by building equipment for submarines in greater quantity than ever before. "We are more determined today than ever to see that the machinery the Navy has asked for is delivered on time in the quantities needed."[104]

Representing the employees at the plant, C.A. Josephson, a longtime employee and president of the local United Steel Workers of America (USWA), accepted "E" pins on behalf of the employees, declaring that through the cooperation of employees and management, they had been successful in the production of war materials that far exceeded the normal volume of scheduled work. "All of us carry with us in our daily work a vision of a man on the front line who is contributing his time, his effort, and his life toward attainment of victory."[105]

Hubbard noted that more and more reports were surfacing regarding the heroic exploits of submarines attached to U.S. fleets, "many of which are powered by electrical equipment built right here in this shop."[106]

In 1959, while visiting Bill Jackson in San Diego, California, a navy man who had been a Japanese prisoner of war (his story of survival is in a later chapter), Winslow Smith, who was employed at the Elliott Company in 1943 and was still in its employ in 1959 as part of its electrical maintenance crew, toured an aircraft carrier and a submarine. The submarine was powered by Elliott Company motors, and Smith was given a close-up look at the machinery still in use that had been manufactured in Ridgway.

National Munitions Plant, Eldred, Pennsylvania

One Killed in Explosion at Eldred Plant
Detonators Explode in Field 2,000 Ft. from Buildings
No Others Endangered

John Paul Breck, 26, of Reynoldsville, an employee of the National Munitions company plant at Eldred, was killed today while disposing of rejected detonators.

Premature explosion of the detonators killed him instantly. He was 2,000 feet from the nearest plant building at the time, and no other plant workers were endangered, plant officials said.

Breck, a foreman of one of the plant buildings, had carried the detonators to what is known as the "proof plot" and was believed preparing to explode them when the premature blast occurred. A plant guard, John Brooks, witnessed the explosion but was unable to throw any light on its cause.

He said his attention was attracted by the blast and a cloud of dust rising from the ground, and that Breck was dead when he arrived on the scene.

Coroner Thomas Clark, of Bradford, was conducting an investigation for the county. He said the explosion occurred at 11:05 a.m.

Breck had been living in Olean since working at the munitions plant.

Several more residents of Mt. Jewett and Kane are employed at the National Munitions plant, most of them commuting by company bus.[107]

Eldred is a small community located in McKean County. One of its main attractions is the Eldred World War II Museum, which features a half dozen large rooms filled with thousands of items from the war. What many people may not know about Eldred is that it was the site of the National Munitions Plant during the war. The museum tells the story of that community's involvement in the war while also telling the larger story of the war. The museum has more than ten thousand books related to the war and has interviews with more than four thousand veterans.[108]

A site was chosen about four miles from Eldred Borough as the location for the National Munitions Plant. That plant covered approximately two thousand acres of land in an area known as the Big Loop and Little Loop Hollows. In 1941, the plant was an operating loading plant for mortar shells, incendiary grenades, thermite aerial bombs and bomb fuses. Owned by Great Britain, it was incorporated in 1941. From 1941 through 1945, 8 million devices were produced there.

The plant, which employed 1,500 people, got its start when a prominent Cleveland attorney, George Roudebush, received a request from the British government to find a site to build a munitions plant to support the war effort. Roudebush first turned his attention to Canada but failed to find a suitable location. Knowing that explosives were already in use in McKean County for oil and gas exploration, and because of the county's remote location, he began to look for a site there.

Successful in securing a location, construction of Plant 1 was started in February 1941 and completed in August. This was no small undertaking. The large complex housed more than fifty structures, including a large guardhouse, two huge warehouses, administration buildings, a hospital unit and testing grounds. Of the 1,500 people employed there, 95 percent were housewives, as most men had been called into the military.[109]

In January 1942, shortly after the attack on Pearl Harbor, the National Munitions Plant was advertising for women between the ages of eighteen and fifty to apply for jobs described as light assembly work and inspection. To get the employees to work, it was arranged for six buses a day to travel between Bradford and the plant in Eldred.

In an interview with the *Bradford Era* in 2014, one woman who had worked at the factory recalled her experiences there when she was seventeen years old. Geraldine Zetler started work there in the summer of 1943 after graduating from high school. "We carpooled to get to work, because there were gas rations," she remembered. Many of the people working at the plant were neighbors and friends supporting the war effort. Most had family members serving in the armed forces.

Zetler recalled, "There were special rubber buttons on our outfits," and the workers wore special turbans on their heads, precautions taken to lessen the chance of static electricity being created, which would have led to an explosion.[110]

Some of Zetler's duties included loading empty shell casings on the conveyer belt and riveting tails onto the incendiary bombs. Employees made thirty-five to fifty cents per hour, with specialized work paying up to seventy cents per hour. Her aunt worked in Plant 1, where the people were paid more; employees working there happened to get yellow skin and were known as "canary girls," a nickname associated with the female workers that dated back to munitions production during World War I.[111]

When asked about the dangers of working in the plant, Zetler said, "We knew there was a danger, but didn't worry about it because we weren't any worse off than they were, meaning the men fighting the war."[112]

The plant, which was shut down in October 1946, was slowly dismantled, and few traces remain today. In 1994, Thomas Roudebush, son of George Roudebush, built a free Christian summer camp for inner-city youth called Camp Penuel East at the location of the former plant.[113]

Zippo Manufacturing Company, Bradford, Pennsylvania

Ernest Taylor Pyle, or Ernie Pyle as he was known affectionately to millions of readers during World War II, was a war correspondent who had worked for the Scripps-Howard newspaper syndicate from 1935 to 1941. Known for his folksy way of telling the stories of ordinary people, once the United States entered the war, he became a war correspondent. His human-interest stories centered on his wartime reports on location from Europe and the Pacific. He was killed by enemy fire during the Battle of Okinawa.

You may be wondering what Ernie Pyle had to do with Zippo. Well, for one thing, he wrote about the company and its lighters:

> *The Zippo Manufacturing Co., of Bradford, PA, makes Zippo cigarette lighters. In peacetime they are nickel-plated and shiny. In wartime they are black, with a rough finish.*
>
> *Zippos are not available at all to civilians. In Amry P.X.'s all around the world, where a batch comes in occasionally, there are long waiting lists.*
>
> *Well, some months ago I had a letter from the president of the Zippo Company. It seems he is devoted to this column. It seems further that he'd had an idea. He has sent to our headquarters in Washington to get my signature and then he was having the signature engraved on a special nickel-plated lighter and he is going to send it to me as a gift.*
>
> *Pretty soon there was another letter. The president of the Zippo Company had had another brainstorm. In addition to my super-heterodyne lighter he was going to send 50 of the regular ones for me to give to friends.*
>
> *I was amused at the modesty of the president's letter. He said, "You probably know nothing about the Zippo lighter."*

War correspondent Ernie Pyle at Anzio, Italy, 1944. *Wikimedia Commons.*

If he only knew how the soldiers covet them. They'll burn in the wind, and pilots say they are the only kind that will light at extreme altitudes. Why, they're so popular I've had three of them stolen from me in the past year.

Well, at last the lighters have come, forwarded all the way from Italy. My own lighter is a beauty, with my name on one side and a little American flag on the other. I'm smoking twice as much as usual just because I enjoy lighting the thing.

Black finish Zippo lighter. *Wikimedia Commons.*

The 50 others are going like hot cakes. I find myself equipped with a wonderful weapon for winning friends and influencing people. Thanks from all of us, Mr. Zippo.[114]

The Zippo Manufacturing Company had its beginnings at the Bradford Country Club in the 1930s, when its founder, George G. Blaisdell, watched a friend struggle to use an Austrian-made lighter. Blaisdell noted that the lighter had a unique chimney that worked well in the wind, but the lighter itself was of poor design, requiring the use of two hands. Flimsily made, its thin metal surface was easily dented.

In 1932, Blaisdell went to work on a new design, incorporating the chimney design that protected the flame into a small rectangular case with an attached lid with hinge. The result was an attractive lighter that operated with one hand. As far as the name Zippo goes, it is reported Blaisdell like the word *zipper* and tried variations until he came up with Zippo.

The new lighter sold for $1.95 and was backed by an unconditional lifetime guarantee. The company filed for a patent in 1934, and it was granted in 1936.[115] Those who favor Zippo lighters over others recognize the distinctive click that is made upon opening the lid.

When the United States entered World War II, Zippo ceased production of lighters for consumer markets and dedicated its production to the U.S. military. The military-style Zippo lighter featured its familiar steel case but made with a black crackle finish. Supplying the military market brought full production for the plant. At the end of the war in 1945, Zippo returned to selling lighters to peacetime America.[116]

In 1945, following the death of Ernie Pyle, the Bradford newspaper reported a story in his memory:

900 ZIPPO LIGHTERS SENT TO MEN ON ERNIE PYLE'S SHIP

"In Memory of Ernie Pyle, 1945"

That inscription is contained on each of 900 Zippo lighters being mailed today by George Blaisdell, president of the Zippo Manufacturing Co., to the captain of the flat top on which Ernie Pyle was stationed during his Pacific tour of duty.

Previous to Pyle's death, Mr. Blaisdell mailed the Era war correspondent 100 lighters monthly to be distributed free to men in combat.

The shipment of 900 lighters will be distributed to the men assigned to the carrier on which Ernie served.[117]

Zippo lighters are highly prized collectibles, and the company has many versions on display at the Zippo/Case Museum in Bradford, including the first pocket Zippo, produced in 1933.

Pennsylvania Ordnance Works, Lycoming County, Pennsylvania

The Manhattan Project was the code name for a highly classified program for America to develop a functional atomic weapon. It was established after U.S. intelligence reported that scientists working for Adolf Hitler were on their way to developing a nuclear weapon, sparking fears that Hitler was prepared to use the weapon in war. The work on the project was conducted in Los Alamos, New Mexico, from 1942 to 1946. Led by the United States in collaboration with the United Kingdom and Canada, it involved some of the world's leading scientific minds, as well as the U.S. military.

During World War II, the federal government spent $50 million to build a highly classified facility in southern Lycoming County to manufacture TNT. Recent research reveals that the Pennsylvania Ordnance Works was used for more than making ammunition.

White Deer Valley is located in a remote region of Lycoming County. During the Revolutionary War, White Deer Valley was home to the widow Catherine Smith, mother of ten children and owner of three hundred acres of land. She first operated a gristmill, but in the summer of 1776, she built a large boring mill where gun barrels were bored for use in the Revolutionary War. It was the only factory of its kind in that section of the state. During the Revolution, her mills were burned by Indians, causing her to flee.[118] Mrs. Smith is remembered to this day with a historical marker, "Catherine's Crown," located near her mills. After a small change in boundary lines, her mills are now located in Union County.

In 1942, the federal government bought or condemned 8,400 acres of land in southern Lycoming and northern Union Counties for construction of an ordnance works and access to the Susquehanna River.

In a review of records in recent years, it was revealed that the government acquired 163 family farms and 47 other properties, destroyed 580 buildings and displaced about 400 residents because of the need for TNT for World War II.[119]

Industrial engineers at the DuPont Company designed the manufacturing facilities for the Ordnance Department, and the U.S. Army Corps of Engineers supervised construction of the plant. Work was begun at the Allenwood area of White Deer Valley in April 1942. TNT production began in February 1943, less than fourteen months after the attack on Pearl Harbor.[120]

Roads, a water supply, power, heat, adequate disposal systems, communications services, hospitals and fire stations were also constructed as part of the facility. Precautions were taken to use only the minimum of critical war materials, avoiding what was referred to as "construction luxuries."[121]

At one point, the Pennsylvania Ordnance Works made an appeal for one hundred women to be trained for laboratory technical work, setting up a special women's industrial relations department, believed to be unique in American industry. The women were trained at Williamsport's Dickinson-Junior College. The women who satisfactorily completed the nine-week course would qualify for work in the Pennsylvania Ordnance Works laboratory.[122]

The plant had two separate divisions of production, one for acid and one for TNT production. TNT, the major product of the plant, was one of the most destructive weapons of war and yet was one of the safest explosives to be manufactured. TNT was used in a number of ways by the military, including for demolition purposes in bombs dropped from airplanes or in projectiles fired through torpedo tubes or cannons.[123]

The plant was guarded against intrusions, fire and sabotage by a semi-military patrol and protection service.[124] In 1944, officials of the Army Third Service Command, the Army Ordnance and the United States Rubber Company, which managed the plant, presented the Army "E" Award for efficiency to the plant's guard force. Lieutenant Colonel A.W. Morgan, commanding officer of the Internal Security Third District, Third Service

Command, in making the presentation of the award, complimented the plant guards on the excellent job they had done in furnishing a high degree of protective security at the Pennsylvania Ordnance Works.[125]

But the operation of the plant was short-lived. On January 20, 1944, just several days after the plant security guard received its "E" Award on January 8, it was announced that production of TNT at the Pennsylvania Ordnance Works would be closed—not just the White Deer Valley plant but also the Keystone Ordnance Works at Meadville, Pennsylvania, and the Waldon Spring Ordnance Works at Waldon Spring, Missouri. The following explanation was given for closing the plants: "Due to the great efficiency of our ordnance high explosive manufacturing plants, it becomes necessary for us to reduce the production of TNT. The requirements for TNT are fixed by the army supply program, which in turn is based upon changing battle conditions. Consequently, it becomes necessary to discontinue the production of TNT at the Pennsylvania Ordnance Works at the close of operations January 16, 1944."[126] The headline in the article announcing the plant closing noted that the plant at White Deer Valley would be kept in "standby" condition.

So, what does that have to do with the Manhattan Project? A local historian, Stephen C. Huddy, determined that the Pennsylvania Ordnance Works was used for more than making munitions—under top-secret conditions, fifty tons of uranium metal turnings in 1943 and 1944 were stored in sealed drums in 4 of the 150 concrete igloos that had been built to house the TNT produced at the plant.[127]

Huddy stated that he was shocked to find out that the uranium waste had been shipped across the country from New Mexico, where the Manhattan Project experiments were taking place. Through his research, he found documents that showed that in 1943, when production of TNT at the plant began, thirty-six barrels of uranium turnings totaling 19,211 pounds were received at the ordnance in September. A second shipment of 17,000 pounds of radioactive debris was received in the next three to four weeks after the first shipment. A final shipment was received on April 26, 1944, eleven days after the Pennsylvania Ordnance Works had been decommissioned. Eventually, the waste was removed. It remains unclear if any of the drums holding the radioactive material were ever unsealed on site.[128]

When Huddy began his research into the facility in 2013, he found that the remnants of buildings and foundations of homes remained scattered in the vegetation on land the government deeded to other entities, including

4,200 acres to the U.S. Bureau of Prisons, where it built the Allenwood prison; 3,018 acres went to the Game Commission; 220 acres were sold to Lycoming County; and 400 acres were given for use as a campus for an earth sciences program.[129]

In May 2011, Pennsylvania's Department of Environmental Protection, through its Bureau of Radiation, performed radiation scans on roadways on state game land. The scans found no indication of uranium or other radioactive elements "above natural background levels." According to the Department of Environmental Protection, the Bureau of Prisons did not permit scans of two igloos on its land.[130]

Neither the workers making TNT nor the public knew that the ordnance works was being used as a radioactive waste dump. Despite the government's promise that it would return the land that was taken to its owners after it was no longer needed for the war effort, the majority of original landowners were never given an opportunity to reclaim their properties.[131] Both the village and the ordnance have vanished.

Piper Aircraft Corporation, Lock Haven, Pennsylvania

Piper Aircraft has been in business since 1937, when William T. Piper, one of the heads of the Taylor Aircraft Company in Bradford, Pennsylvania, purchased the company shares of joint owner Gilbert Taylor. Piper renamed the aircraft company, and in March 1937, after a fire destroyed the Bradford facility, Piper moved it to an abandoned silk mill in Lock Haven.

When the United States entered World War II in 1941, more than 60 percent of U.S. registered civilian light aircraft were Piper Cubs. The armed forces used thousands of various Cubs for reconnaissance, ambulance and supply transport aircraft. By the end of the war, 75 percent of all Civilian Pilot Training Program pilots had been trained on a Piper Cub.[132]

William Piper, the owner of the company, made a prediction about the Cubs only hours after the attack on Pearl Harbor: "They will have their place in the war." In short time, the U.S. Army Air Force ordered 1,500 Grasshoppers along with training of field artillery pilots. This training gave rise to army ground force aviation, where a single man in a small plane could influence the course of battle. Improved Grasshoppers were soon being manufactured, including ambulance planes for the navy and glider trainers. They were first used in combat during the invasion of North Africa, when three took off from a carrier for reconnaissance.[133]

Piper Grasshopper. *Wikimedia Commons.*

Eventually, the Grasshopper operated with the U.S. Army in every campaign of the war. During the invasion of Sicily and Italy, Grasshopper pilots directed fire over the beaches. General Mark Clark used his Grasshopper to inspect the battlefront at Anzio. During the invasion of Normandy, Grasshoppers directed firings at fortifications along the beaches. In his personal Grasshopper, Dwight Eisenhower inspected the battle areas. As Patton's tanks raced toward Germany, Grasshoppers added bazookas to their planes to knock out tanks and entrenched artillery.[134]

In the Pacific, Grasshoppers went directly against Japanese strongholds, directing artillery against them and providing support in the campaigns from New Guinea to the Philippines.[135]

In a 1944 newspaper article published in Lock Haven, it was disclosed that the Nazis feared the small airplanes, with one officer referring to them as "Hell Raisers":

> *Germans Fear Cubs, Knowing They Mean Artillery Fire*
> *It is a helpless little plane, without armament and with a fuselage a fist can punch through. In a strong wind, it has been known to hover above the ground at a speed of 15 miles an hour.*

> *Yet, the War Department disclosed, the name the Germans have given it is the "Hell Raiser."*
>
> *In their gun pits and foxholes on the Italian front, the enemy cowers when one of these Cubs wings overhead. There are few things they dread more than these "Hell Raisers," the tiny Piper planes employed by American artillery for air observation and the spotting of Enemy positions. For they know that close behind their appearance will come a rain of incredibly accurate and deadly steel from the other side of the mountain or ravine*
>
> *A German officer, wounded and captured, apprised the Americans of the name given these Piper Cubs, powered by a 65-horsepower engine and manned by a crew of two. "We call them Hell Raisers" he explained while convalescing in an American hospital behind the lines "after our unteroffizier von Dienst—the duty officer who inspects our barracks every day and always raises hell when he sees something that displeases him."*
>
> *Once, only a few minutes after one of the observation planes had appeared in the sky over the lines, a moving German convoy was destroyed by American gunfire. On another occasion, a concentration of Nazi troops and material was broken up after one of the feared little planes slipped from behind a mountain and detected it....*
>
> *The flyers and the artillerymen they assist are agreed on one point: The Hell Raisers were aptly named by the wounded German officer—wounded by the gunfire they directed.*[136]

The Piper Aircraft Corporation was ahead of its time in some respects. One woman, Alma Heslin, was a test pilot for Piper. It was said that in 1942, she was the only female test pilot in the world. From her physical appearance, she would not have been taken for an experienced pilot. A soft-spoken woman, she weighed 110 pounds and looked much younger than her thirty years. She and another woman employed at Piper at one point flew to Alaska and back to Seattle in a 1940 Piper Cub coupe.[137]

In 1943, W.T. Piper attended the Army Women Airforce Service Pilots (WASP) graduation at Sweetwater, Texas. He said, "Women and light airplanes started off together in this war. The Army Air Forces could see no need for either. But now the Cub 'grasshopper' has proved its liaison value in every theater of war and the WASPs trained in Texas have won the admiration of all by their fine noncombatant flying record."[138] Piper noted his support for women who wanted to learn to fly. The company sponsored the Cub Flier's Club for Piper employees and had 107 women in its membership of 226. The club's service flag had more than three hundred stars, with twenty-two representing girls who were enrolled in the WASP program.[139]

In 2018, at the annual Piper Club fly-in in Lock Haven, Clinton County, Pennsylvania, Piper Museum President John Bryerton noted the importance of the Grasshoppers used during World War II: "They could land in fields and report to our troops, refuel, go again."[140]

Sherwood Refining Company and Struthers-Wells, Warren, Pennsylvania

Warren, in Warren County, is located near the birthplace of the oil industry and today remains a major refining area in the Wilds. In World War II, the histories of two companies—Sherwood Refining Company and Struthers-Wells Corporation—make for interesting reading.

Oil from Pennsylvania is unlike oil from Texas and other western states. Pennsylvania's crude is green, developed from rotting green plants, while western oil is tar based. Visiting an oil well in the region, one can observe a yellowish gel at the well site known as paraffin, an undesirable product that fouls machinery. Enter a man named Sherwood, a local businessman. Sherwood had done his homework and knew that the yellow gel could be easily refined and turned into a clear, odorless compound, petroleum jelly, what people commonly refer to today by the brand name Vaseline. Sherwood decided that he could make a fortune selling refined paraffin. World War II offered him the perfect opportunity, as the U.S. military was looking for products that could treat wounds and burns. At the peak of his business, Sherwood employed sixty employees.[141] A photo on a modern website shows the image of a tin can that once contained Sherwood's product, labeled Sherolatum Petrolatum Petroleum Jelly Tin, Sherwood Refining, Warren, Pennsylvania. Sherwood produced his jelly by the carloads, shipping it by rail to other companies for marketing.

Struthers-Wells was a steel forging, fabricating, welding and engineering facility experienced in the production of standard and special processing equipment for the chemical and related process industries, marine and diesel crankshaft forgings, steering gears, windlasses, capstans and winches and steel boilers of all types.[142]

With the outbreak of the war, one Struthers-Wells official proclaimed, "We are unreservedly pledged to a 'Win the War Program'...our 'all-out' effort is being expended in but one direction…to produce the absolute maximum in the shortest possible time and to devote every ton of our capacity to America's most vital war needs."[143]

Prior to the war, production equipment and facilities of the company included forging presses up to two thousand tons in size, lathes one hundred feet long, 172 welding machines and three complete machine shops. With three locations—Titusville Forge Division and Titusville Iron Division, along with the local Struthers-Wells Division in Warren—the company moved out of its peacetime production of producing standard and special processing equipment for the metallurgical industry; manufacture of oils, fats and soap; paint, varnish and lacquer industries; byproduct, coke and gas industries; processing of plastics and insulations; rubber industry; sugar industry; textile, bleaching and finishing industries; ice and refrigeration industry; paper and pulp industries; and fire and water tube boilers for both heating and power.

During the war years, "It participated in defense programming, fabricating hundreds of heat exchangers and condensers for Liberty Gun Ships and gun mounts.…It employed over 1,000 in Warren County and nearly 5,000 between the shops in Titusville and Warren."[144]

In a special ceremony in November 1942, Struthers-Wells employees were awarded Army-Navy "E" pins, and the "E" flag was flown over the plant. The awards were for high achievement in the production of war equipment. The Struthers-Wells band, made up of forty-five members, played several selections during the ceremony, which was attended by military officers, employees (including seven who had more than forty years of service with the company) and many local and civic business officials. It was reported that "the award recognized the exceptional performance on the production front, of the determined, persevering, unbeatable American spirit which can be satisfied only by achieving today what yesterday seemed impossible."[145]

Part IV

THE HOMEFRONT

NEWS FROM THE *BROCKWAY RECORD*

The *Brockway Record* was a hometown newspaper that was owned by the Durbin family for a number of years. The newspaper was operating prior to and during World War II and often reported news of its current and former residents.

Elsa Youngdahl

In 1941, the newspaper reported on the evacuation of Miss Elsa Youngdahl, a hometown girl, from Singapore, which had fallen to the Japanese:

> *FLASH FROM CHINA*
> *Mr. and Mrs. Hugo Youngdahl, after several days of anxiety, received on Wednesday evening a cablegram sent the evening of Dec. 16 from their daughter Elsa with the one word, "Safe." Miss Youngdahl is a teaching missionary, located in Singapore on the Malaya peninsula, and when news of the bombing of Singapore was received her family and friends were naturally apprehensive and we rejoice with the family in tidings of her safety.*[146]

Elsa Youngdahl was born in Brockport, Elk County, Pennsylvania, in 1910. Her father was born in Sweden and her mother in Ridgway, Elk County. She attended State Teachers College at Indiana, which today is Indiana University of Pennsylvania (IUP).

In February 1935, while working in the public school at Brockway, she resigned her position to accept an appointment as an English teacher in the Singapore schools under the Board of Missions of the Methodist Episcopal Church.[147]

Youngdahl, later speaking about her experiences in Singapore, painted a picture of the strategic position of Singapore and the important products from the Peninsula, including growing rubber and bananas and mining tin.

Elsa Youngdahl. *Indiana State Teachers College, 1930.*

Youngdahl recounted that while Singapore was prepared for war, it was also unprepared for what happened. Although the populace had been subjected to air raids, shelter zones and blackout drills, when the siege by the Japanese began, many bombs were dropped on the civilian areas. As the Japanese invaded in the north, hundreds of refugees traveled to Singapore for safety, which cut into the meager rations of food and fuel for the citizens of Singapore.[148]

Singapore was known as the "Gibraltar of the East" and was a strategic British stronghold in Asia. It had been a British colony since the nineteenth century. In July 1941, as the Japanese made advances against French Indochina, they also let it be known that they were going to be adding Singapore to their ever-growing empire. On the eve of the December 7, 1941 attack on Pearl Harbor, twenty-four thousand Japanese troops were transported to the Malay Peninsula. The initial attack by Japanese fighter pilots killed sixty-one Singapore civilians by air. The battle between the British and Japanese continued through December and January, with many more civilians killed in the process. In February, Japanese troops landed onto Singapore Island, and by February 13, Singapore's main defensive weapons, fifteen-inch coastal guns, had been destroyed. The British surrendered to the Japanese on February 15, 1942, with sixty-two thousand Allied soldiers taken prisoner. More than half of them died as prisoners of war.[149]

Youngdahl narrowly missed the fall of Singapore, having escaped from the Malay Peninsula on January 30, 1942, by way of Batavia (which today is Jakarta, Indonesia) to Melbourne, Australia, and finally to San Francisco. It wasn't until January 1, 1943, that she learned the fate of several of her friends. Escaping after the fall of Singapore on February 15, 1942, they secured small yachts and drifted around and were gradually smuggled to places of safety. Youngdahl noted that she would be returning to her missionary work once the Allies won the war.[150]

Dear Ralph

Ralph Durbin, son of the owners of the *Brockway Record*, wrote "Soldiers News" in the local paper, reporting such things as addresses for the local servicemen. He also started a sub-column titled "Dear Ralph," which was popular among those serving in the armed forces as they were writing letters home. The letters to Ralph shed light on the day-to-day activities in the lives of the servicemen from locations all across the world. The following is a sampling of those letters.

With Charles Poyer in North Africa, June 4, 1943:

> *Hello, Ralph: I suppose you are wondering why I'm writing to you now when I never did before. I just thought you liked news!*
>
> *Well, I have been here in Africa for quite some time now, and every time we move I find something interesting and different.*
>
> *I have been in the city of Bone, Algiers, and also the city of Constantine. Both of these are very beautifully planned and set cities and the buildings are quite like those of our small city buildings. It is mostly run by the French, which is the master language, and also thickly populated by the Arab, which is the low class of people who will work his head off for a good American cigarette.*
>
> *The main work here seems to be fruit growing and agriculture, horses, cattle and sheep raising. They have some very beautiful horses over here. Most of them seem to be thoroughbred and really are built for speed.*
>
> *If I wish I can go to a movie, but it's all in French and quite hard to understand, but as I progress, my French vocabulary broadens and I am now able to speak in short phrases, very choppy, but I get by.*
>
> *I am hoping this war will be at an end soon and the lights will again rule the streets, then we boys will return to our regular mode of life again.*
>
> *Well, I'll close now and hoping to hear from you and the Record. Good Luck.*
>
> *Your friend, Pvt. Charles L. Poyer*[151]

Location: Ellis, Illinois, November 5, 1943:

Dear Ralph: I'm a cook in this man's army—but, by gosh, hang cooking when I've a Brockway Record to read. Actually the paper is such a welcome thing to me that I'd let my cooking go in the capable hands of my second, third and fourth cook while I stop to read the latest news—especially the soldiers' news. And you've heard that next to food a soldier wants mail so you can see just how much I appreciate the home town paper.

As I just said, I'm a cook. My three-and-a-half years of college evidently gives me the right background to being a cook. Uncle Bob (Warren) always told me I'd never be satisfied in life unless I was messing around in a kitchen—and he sure was right! You'd be surprised how much fun it is breaking two cases of eggs (approximately 720 eggs) alone or mixing up 25 or 30 gallons of pancake batter using five pounds of baking powder instead of the customary four teaspoons full.

I could tell you the Thanksgiving menu for all men in the Army. It is roast turkey (the master menu calls for one pound of turkey per man), mashed potatoes, giblet gravy, cranberry sauce, dressing, tomatoes and lettuce salad, buttered rolls, fresh peas, celery, olives, nuts, pumpkin pie and coffee. So, you people at home shouldn't worry about your sons and friends going hungry on Thanksgiving Day. By the way, I suspect you've heard about the awful meals soldiers get in the Army. The only answer I have to that is what the private in the bunk next to mine wrote home: "The meals we get in this company are just like poison to me-besides the portions are so small." Get what I mean?

I get a kick out of reading the letters a lot of the boys write. A good many say something about gaining so many extra pounds is decidedly funny for me because I've been in the service for 13 months and have had access to all the food and deserts I want, yet I've gained but four pounds and seven ounces in all that time. And cooks are rumored to be big and fat!

I keep watching the addresses column for fellows stationed in Illinois at my camp (Camp Ellis, Illinois), but evidently everyone has had better luck than I and got stationed at good camps. Where is Franklin Buskirk stationed nowadays? I'd sure appreciate his address if you have it.

By the way, my new address is PFC. George H. Gillung, ASN 130-93037, 582 Salv. And Rpr. Bn. Camp Ellis, Illinois. And I suspect even this address will be changed soon, but I'll let you know.

A Brockway soldier, George Gillung.

Location in the States undisclosed, published on November 12, 1943:

Dear Ralph: I'm on the last break before the last problem of these maneuvers, so I thought I'd write and give you an idea of what it's like.

The weather is altogether different than what "Swamp Rabbit" said it was last summer. It's really cold. We sleep on one blanket on the ground. Usually two or three of us pool our blankets and sleep in the same "bed." We are all soaked in the morning from the dew, which you would call a light rain up north.

We eat practically with no lights at five-yard intervals about 10 at night and get to bed—that is if we are not out on security. Breakfast is at 4 or 4:30 a.m. and draw lunches for dinner which consists of one jelly and one cheese sandwich, an apple or orange. We are on the go all day on various problems, attacking, defending, maneuvering, walking or digging in which is a "must" out here. Our foxholes are 2 ½ by 3 ½ and six feet down. Tell Doc we have some fine clay down here.

We have a three-day problem and a three-day break. These breaks are really nice. We have field PXs and occasionally a movie.

This all sounds tough and is tough, but it is a picnic compared to what some of our buddies are doing overseas.

Will soon hit a camp in Texas and from there I don't know where I'll be.

Mom sends me the Record so I'm pretty well informed on what's going on back there. Keep it up, Ralph, a lot of boys are counting on you.

Yours, "Tony" Thompson[152]

Location: Northern Ireland, published on January 28, 1944:

Dear Ralph and All: Well I guess you have had a letter from about every one of the boys from Brockway who left to serve in the armed forces but me, so having a few spare minutes at this time, I thought I would write you a few lines.

This finds me at this writing somewhere in Northern Ireland and I find the people and the country very interesting and like it quite well especially their Irish brogue, but it rains here almost every day and that is not so good as it makes it too wet and damp.

If it is possible I would like you to send me the Record. I had been receiving it for awhile but for some reason it was discontinued. I surely enjoy reading the home town news and would be very glad to get the Record again.

Now, I must close. Tell your mother and all my friends hello for me. I trust this finds you all well and happy and may God's richest blessing be yours.

Your friend in Christ,
Pvt. Don Maxwell
Corinthians 15:57: But thanks be unto God Who giveth us the victory through our Lord Jesus Christ.[153]

Location: Tehran, Iran, March 3, 1944:

Dear Ralph: Have some spare time so I decided to write you a short letter.

We are now allowed to mention that we are located at or rather near Teheran, the largest and most modern city of Iran. It is also the capital city of this country.

I visit Teheran about every six weeks, as there is nothing there that interests me.

We have a very nice camp and with a nice and large enlisted men's service club. We boys spend much of our off-duty hours there.

My wishes are that everyone in Brockway and vicinity are enjoying good health.

We boys know and appreciate the good job everyone is doing on the home front.

Although I receive the Brockway paper quite some time after it is issued, I certainly enjoy it and read it through carefully. I believe I can speak for all of us boys in service and with that the page for the letters and addresses of those in service are very much appreciated.

Am enclosing a clipping from our command paper concerning a little information of the work of our organization. Thought maybe you would care to read it.

I am in the best of health and waiting word to sail to good old USA.

Please give my best regards to all.

Wishing you and your family health and happiness.

As ever, Friend, Bill Daughenbaugh[154]

Day-to-Day Life

Can you imagine the fear that gripped the country in the early days after the attack on Pearl Harbor and the U.S. declaration of war against Japan and Germany?

Once the United States entered the war, Germany sent U-boats into American waters. Their goal was to destroy merchant cargo vessels up and down the East Coast and the Caribbean, cutting Europe off from materials from America. In the Pacific, Japanese submarines reached the Philippines and attacked Fort Stevens in Oregon and the Elwood oil field near Santa Barbara, California. They invaded Alaskan islands and bombed a harbor in Alaska.[155]

The United States had to quickly mobilize itself for war. People moved around the country to take on newly created defense jobs, while others moved to begin military training.

One important action was the formation of a Civil Defense Force, which actually was underway in Pennsylvania in March 1941, prior to the country's entrance in the war, possibly because of the gathering war clouds with Europe already heavily involved in war. The Civil Defense Force initially was set at 1,934 officers and men.[156]

Following the attack on Pearl Harbor, 101 people registered for Civil Defense work in Bellefonte, Pleasant Gap and Milesburg in Centre County at a special day held on Saturday, December 27, 1941. This special registration expanded the Civil Defense Council to approximately 500 people in the Bellefonte district.[157]

All across the Wilds region, people stepped up to provide defense services. In Wellsboro, Tioga County, just three days after Pearl Harbor, on December 10, 1941, an emergency meeting was called looking for volunteers to serve as air raid wardens.[158]

"Let 'em Come!" *National Archives.*

Civil Defense volunteers learned to identify planes by sight and sound, and they enforced blackout mandates during air raid siren drills. Civil Defense officials began conducting dusk-to-dawn blackouts across the Wilds region. One such blackout took place from 8:30 p.m. until 5:00 a.m. the next morning. "The start of the 30 minute 'total' blackout will be signaled by air raid sirens at some time during the night, the exact time being a secret until the warning is given. During this total blackout period defense officials have particularly urged people to avoid all unnecessary phone calls. Telephone channels must be kept open for the instant and uninterrupted use of Army and Navy and civilian fire, police and air raid chiefs and plane spotters during any kind of an air raid, it was emphasized."[159]

Newspapers ran advertisements on how to prepare one's home for air raids and blackouts, with drawings showing blackout blinds on a living room window while the inhabitants of the house went about their normal activities, with an article about blackouts noting that "we are compelled to learn how to keep up our normal life in semi-darkness. That is the purpose of the dusk-to-dawn practice blackout."[160]

As men were required for the military, women stepped into the workforce in great numbers, taking over jobs that had been almost exclusively held by men. By the mid-1940s, women in the U.S. workforce had increased from 25 percent to 36 percent. Nearly one out of every four married women worked outside the home.

American moviegoers saw a steady stream of war-related programming. Going to the movies in those war years also meant watching a newsreel, which was loaded with images and accounts of recent battles, prior to the theater running the movie. Even music became war-related, with popular songs like "Praise the Lord and Pass the Ammunition" and "Coming In on a Wing and a Prayer" among others.[161]

Increasingly, people depended on radio for news of the conflict abroad, listening to popular broadcasters such as Edward R. Murrow and reading the writings of war correspondent Ernie Pyle.

Rationing

There were calls early on by the government for the populace of the country to "Do with less—so they'll have enough," referring to supplying U.S. troops with needed food, clothing, fuel oil and more. In the spring of

1942, a rationing program was instituted that set limits on gas, food and clothing consumers could purchase. Ration stamps were issued to families, and individuals conducted drives to collect scrap metal, aluminum cans and rubber, all of which were recycled and used to produce armaments.[162]

Many residents of the Wilds found themselves involved in gardening at the urging of President Roosevelt:

> *In his message to congress on the food program President Roosevelt said: "Much credit is due to the patriotic men and women who spent so much time and energy in planting the twenty million Victory Gardens in the United States and helped to meet the food requirements. It is estimated that about eight million tons of food were produced in 1943 in these Victory Gardens."*
>
> *To his press conference, held prior to sending this message, the president said a campaign would be made to get everyone to grow food in his back yard in 1944 and expressed the hope that production would be double that of 1943.*[163]

The numbers reported were staggering. In 1943, more than half of the fresh vegetables available to civilians were grown in Victory Gardens. It was said that on non-farm Victory Gardens, estimated to total 15 million, 3,200,000 tons of vegetables were generated; Victory Gardens on farms, numbering 5 million, produced 4,740,000 tons of vegetables. These figures are in addition to vegetables produced by large-scale vegetable growers.[164]

There were staggering figures reported on Victory Gardens in Punxsutawney, Pennsylvania:

> *WPA Victory Gardens Produce Tons of Needed Vegetables Five Operated Under Direction of Street Commissioner Means—4,000 Quarts Canned by Women for School Lunches*
>
> *Punxsutawney's Victory Gardens, operated by WPA labor under the supervision of Walter Means, borough street commissioner, have produced literally tons of produce, the value of which is inestimable in these war times.*
>
> *Five gardens were operated with seven men working. One garden of two town lots in the Elk Run section produced three tons of cabbage, five bushels of onions. From another corn, cabbage, onions and tomatoes in generous quantities are now being harvested. A third had produced tomatoes in great quantities—another cabbage, beans, carrots, corn and tomatoes. A fifth was devoted entirely to corn, beans and peas.*

Left: "Do with less so they'll have enough!" *Wikimedia Commons.*

Right: "Plant a Victory Garden. Our food is fighting." *Wikimedia Commons.*

> *There is no means yet of determining the total yield but it is enormous, a credit to the men working the gardens and to Mr. Means, who supervised the work.*
>
> *Under the direction of Mrs. George Brady and Mrs. Hugh Curry on another WPA project a considerable portion of this produce and a great quantity of surplus commodities have been canned. Over 4,000 quarts of fruit and vegetables are now in cans and many more quarts will be so preserved when the crops from the victory gardens are all harvested.*
>
> *The fruit and vegetables now in cans and to be canned are being used in dispensing lunches that are served at noon daily in the Jenks Hill and West End Schools.... The 4,000 plus cans of fruit and vegetables are the pride of the PTA and the women who have done the canning.*[165]

In Warren County, it was reported that home canning and drying of fruits and vegetables had been stimulated by the Victory Garden program and that home canners were urged to

> *conserve not only the products of Victory Gardens, but also the fruits and vegetables produced by commercial growers in Pennsylvania. Quoting from*

reports of the Pennsylvania Department of Agriculture, it is pointed out that the commercial tomato, grape, plum and apple crops are especially large this year,[166] *and many of them are ripening several weeks in advance of the usual season. Canning or drying of these crops locally will release transportation facilities for war needs and will ensure a plentiful food supply which will reduce the danger of inflation and the necessity for rationing.*[167]

Rationing involved setting limits on buying high-demand items, with the government issuing rationing books with stamps for certain items to every person, including babies. Food items began to be rationed in May 1942, starting with sugar. By November, coffee had been added to the list, which progressed to eventually include meats, fats, canned fish, cheese and canned milk. Macaroni and cheese became popular nationwide because it was cheap and filling and required few ration points. Kraft sold 50 million boxes of macaroni and cheese during the war.[168]

Tires were rationed just days after Pearl Harbor. In Warren County, by December 31, 1941, official automobile inspection stations had been designated as inspection agents for the local rationing boards. "You

UNITED STATES OF AMERICA
OFFICE OF PRICE ADMINISTRATION

742385 M

WAR RATION BOOK No. 3 *Void if altered*

NOT VALID WITHOUT STAMP

Identification of person to whom issued: PRINT IN FULL

(First name) (Middle name) (Last name)

Street number or rural route

City or post office State

AGE	SEX	WEIGHT	HEIGHT	OCCUPATION
		Lbs.	Ft. In.	

SIGNATURE
(Person to whom book is issued. If such person is unable to sign because of age or incapacity, another may sign in his behalf.)

WARNING
This book is the property of the United States Government. It is unlawful to sell it to any other person, or to use it or permit anyone else to use it, except to obtain rationed goods in accordance with regulations of the Office of Price Administration. Any person who finds a lost War Ration Book must return it to the War Price and Rationing Board which issued it. Persons who violate rationing regulations are subject to $10,000 fine or imprisonment, or both.

OPA Form No. R-130

LOCAL BOARD ACTION

Issued by (Local board number) (Date)

Street address

City State

(Signature of issuing officer)

Ration book. *John Myers.*

are hereby authorized and deputized to inspect old or worn tires upon request of applicants desiring to purchase new tires."[169] Rationing became effective for car and truck tires on January 5, 1942. The tire rationing administrator in Pennsylvania stated, "This is a patriotic duty, and in this way you can help to serve the nation. You will receive no compensation for these inspections, but we are confident that we shall receive one hundred percent support in this endeavor and are counting upon you."[170]

In Wellsboro, Tioga County, the newspaper published regulations for seven types of vehicles that would, in fact, be approved to purchase tires that would be mounted on certain vehicles:

> *(1) Vehicles used by physicians, surgeons, visiting nurses or veterinarians, principally for professional services; (2) Ambulances; (3) Vehicles used exclusively for fire-fighting services, necessary public police services, enforcement of specific laws affecting public health and safety, garbage removal or other sanitation services, or mail delivery; (4) Vehicles with a capacity of ten or more passengers operated exclusively to carry passengers as part of service rendered to the public by a regular transportation system as school buses, or to carry employees to and from any industrial or mining establishment or construction project except when public transportation facilities are readily available; (5) Trucks used exclusively for ice and fuel delivery, transportation of materials for construction and maintenance of public roads, public utilities or production facilities, defense housing and military establishments; trucks used by essential roofing, plumbing, heating and electrical repair service or waste and scrap dealers; by any common carrier, and for transporting raw materials, semi-manufactured goods and finished products—except that no certificates may be issued to transport such raw materials, semi-manufactured or finished goods to the ultimate consumer for personal family or household use; (6) Farm tractors or other farm implements—except automobiles or trucks—for which tires are essential to operate; (7) Industrial, mining and construction equipment—except automobiles and trucks—for which tires are essential to operate.*[171]

If a motorist's vehicle didn't fall into one of those categories, which would have been the average person who owned an automobile, they were notified that they would not be able to purchase new tires and were urged to "stop unnecessary driving immediately and 'double-up' in driving to work."[172] Gasoline ration books were issued.

Americans!

SHARE THE MEAT

as a wartime necessity

To meet the needs of our armed forces and fighting allies, a Government order limits the amount of meat delivered to stores and restaurants.

To share the supply fairly, all civilians are asked to limit their consumption of beef, veal, lamb, mutton and pork to 2½ lbs. per person per week.

YOUR FAIR WEEKLY SHARE

Men, women and children over 12 yrs. old . . . . 2½ *Pounds per week*

Children 6 to 12 yrs. old . . . . 1½ *Pounds per week*

Children under 6 yrs. old . . . . ¾ *Pound per week*

You can add these foods to your share: liver, sweetbreads, kidneys, brains and other variety meats; also poultry and fish.

HELP WIN THE WAR!

Keep within your share

FOODS REQUIREMENT COMMITTEE
War Production Board

Claude R. Wickard
Chairman

OWI Poster No. 10. Additional copies may be obtained upon request from the Division of Public Inquiries, Office of War Information, Washington, D.C.

Kill the

BLACK MARKET

with your Ration Stamps

- Accept no rationed food without giving up ration stamps
- Pay no more than ceiling prices

EMEMBER: IT TAKES TWO TO MAKE A BLACK MARKET

Left: "Americans share the meat." *Wikimedia Commons.*

Below: "Kill the black market with ration stamps." *Wikimedia Commons.*

Early in 1943, the Office of Price Administration implemented meat rationing when it slashed the amount of meat for civilians by nearly 20 percent, with consumers limited to two and a half pounds of meat per person per week.

Also in 1943, the government announced that wartime rationing of shoes made of leather would go into effect, limiting consumers to buying three pairs per person per year.[173]

So many goods used by citizens were subject to rationing in order to fuel the military effort. Creating shortages, black market trading became a reality and thrived with everything from tires to meat being sold by black market operators. A *Pittsburgh Post Gazette* reporter wrote about his experiences with the black market in Jefferson County located in the Pennsylvania Wilds:

> *Cattle raised in Jefferson county evidently have been playing quite a part in the black market in the Pittsburgh area, as told by a reporter in the Pittsburgh Post Gazette Wednesday morning.*
>
> *A story written by one of the Post Gazette reporters was featured on the front page of the paper and the very first sentence was "All I have to do to get into the black market with meat myself is to truck cattle down from Jefferson County."*
>
> *The writer of the story told how he was going into the black market and how he had contacted a man who would be glad to aid the reporter in the slaughtering of the cattle at the price of five dollars a head.…It has been reported that many cattle are being killed in Jefferson County. Just what extent the cattle from this county have been playing in the Pittsburgh black market could not be learned.*
>
> *The Post Gazette reporter turned over his evidence after he collected it in full to the Office of Price Administration in Pittsburgh.*[174]

The Office of Public Administration mounted an aggressive effort to curtail black market activity, including advertising and the creation of pamphlets to inform citizens about the need for rationing and price ceilings.

War Bonds

Financing a war is an expensive proposition, and the United States spent more than $300 billion in the fight (somewhere around $4 trillion in today's dollars).[175]

The government turned to ordinary citizens to help fund the war by offering a series of war bonds. As an example, a buyer could purchase a $25 war bond for $18.75. The government used that money to help pay for tanks, planes, ships and more, everything the military needed to fight. The government offered the bonds as a ten-year investment, after which time the bond could be redeemed for $25, realizing a $6.25 return on the investment.[176]

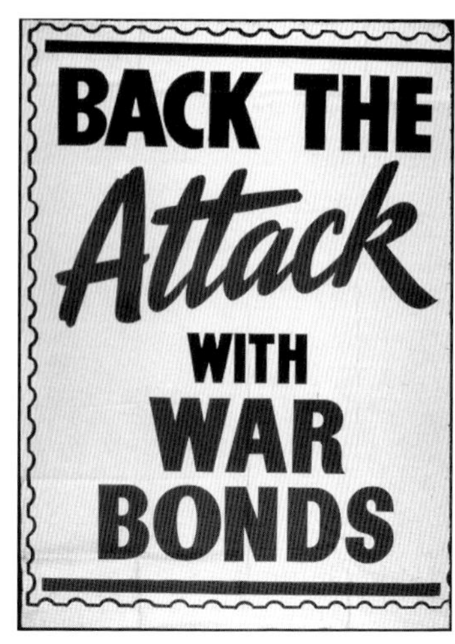

"Back the attack, buy war bonds." *National Archives.*

Newspapers ran advertisements explaining the program, and the public was exposed to posters encouraging the purchase of the bonds. Celebrities like Bob Hope, Frank Sinatra, Bette Davis and Marlene Dietrich traveled the country putting on shows to encourage the purchase of the bonds. Schools held war bond competitions, with students bringing in nickels, dimes and quarters in an effort to out-raise other schools.[177]

One advertisement from the U.S. Treasury Department was titled "Deliver Us from Evil, Buy War Bonds," with the face of a young girl superimposed over a Nazi swastika:

> *Figure It Out Yourself. How can you effectively join in saving all the little children of the world from human slavery, death and injury from the Nazis and Japanese? Put more and more of your pay into war bonds every payday. Your savings will go to war in the form of war equipment and other munitions. How much more should you put into war bonds? The only ones who can answer that are—you and your family. It's up to you to decide just how much more you'll do to win the war.*
>
> *If you were fighting in the Solomons or in Africa or forcing a landing in Europe you'd like to feel that the folks at home were back of you—all the way—you'd be proud of your family and your friends if you knew they were buying war bonds not at 10 percent or 15 percent, but with every cent beyond that which they need for necessities. U.S. Treasury Department.*[178]

Polio Epidemic of 1944

The scourge of the polio epidemic has become a thing of the past since 1954, when Jonas Salk introduced the first polio vaccine. Scientifically known as poliomyelitis or infantile paralysis, it is an infectious virus disease of the central nervous system, sometimes resulting in paralysis. The greatest incidence of the disease was in children between five and ten years of age, but people of any age could be afflicted. It was first recognized in the United States in 1894. After the development and administration of the Salk vaccine, paralytic poliomyelitis declined from 8,308 cases in 1954 to just 61 in 1965.[179]

The symptoms for polio are variable. Mild cases often go undetected. For every paralytic case of polio, there may have been one hundred nonparalytic or asymptomatic cases, with most of them not being recognized as polio. The virus may enter the body through one of several openings, the alimentary tract being probably the most common way. The virus spreads through the blood stream to different parts of the central nervous system. The largest percentage of victims who received proper care recovered with few permanent after effects. However, in severe cases, movement of the diaphragm was affected, and those patients were kept alive via an iron lung machine. The incubation period for polio ranges from about four to thirty-five days.[180]

One of the worst years for polio in Pennsylvania was in 1916, when 2,181 cases were reported, the third most in the country after New York at 13,223 and New Jersey at 4,055.[181] In 1941 and 1943, polio cases were reported throughout the country, but apparently the Wilds region was not affected in those years. But 1944 was different—and, for my family, very personal.

My nine-year-old sister, Elaine Smith, was the second child in Ridgway, Elk County, to come down with polio in September 1944, only a few short weeks after the first case in town in August resulted in the death of Theodore G. Cronk, a seventeen-year-old boy. By October, ten-year-old James Marshall had died from polio at his home. Other children listed with the disease included Ruth Imhof, Ann Marie Murnaghan and John Armanini.

Various actions were taken throughout the Wilds to contain the outbreaks. In Potter County, all public places were ordered closed in August as a preventive measure. That included theaters, churches, schools and fraternal organizations, as well as all other places where large groups would gather.[182]

With steps being taken to contain the epidemic in Tioga County (one of Pennsylvania's smaller and northernmost counties,), by October it was ranked third in the state with 104 polio cases recorded. Philadelphia County was first in the state with 242 confirmed cases, followed by Allegheny County with 139 confirmed cases. The state confirmed a total number of cases in October 25 at 1,338.[183]

The efforts by one community in McKean County in the Wilds to contain the outbreak led to the quarantine of its population of more than one thousand people:

> *All of Ludlow Under Two Week Quarantine*
> *The nearby community of Ludlow with a population of more than 1,000 persons was placed under strict polio quarantine last night which affected every residence and family and also resulted in closing Wildcat Park. County health officers arranged for the quarantine last night which will isolate that community for 14 days.*
>
> *Dr. L.W. Dana, president of the Kane Board of Health stated today there has been no change in the polio situation and that reports of another case at Ludlow were not true. He stated he examined a sick child at that place last night but that there were no symptoms of polio.*
>
> *Condition of Kenneth Thompson, 11, first victim of infantile paralysis at that place, continued serious today. There still was no confirmation of a polio diagnosis in a suspected case at Johnsonburg.*
>
> *As a result of the Ludlow quarantine, no newspaper deliveries are permitted at that place and for the ensuing two weeks copies will be available only at the George W. Beers store.*[184]

DuBois, in Clearfield County, was another community that took steps to stop the spread of polio. Its board of health closed down youth gatherings, barred swimming in all unregistered pools and urged parents not to take their children to other towns or to bring children from other communities

Ludlow Now Under Polio Quarantine

Ludlow under quarantine. *From the* Warren Times Mirror, *August 7, 1944.*

into DuBois. While there were no reported cases in the city at the time these regulations went into effect, the board of health was influenced by several cases that had developed in Ridgway, thirty miles from DuBois—one child had died from the disease, which it was believed he contracted swimming at a pool in a mountain stream near DuBois.[185]

I distinctly remember an old hand ringer machine standing in the attic of the home where I grew up in Ridgway that had an interesting history; it was used to help my sister through her battle with polio. My parents chose to treat Elaine with the controversial Kenny treatment.

Often, the treatment of polio prior to the Kenny method was to place the patients in casts. This resulted in patients eventually wearing leg braces after recovery from the disease. The Kenny treatment took a different approach.

Nine-year-old Elaine Smith with her youngest sibling four months before she contracted polio. *Kathy Myers.*

Elizabeth Kenny was born into a lower-middle-class family in rural Australia and received little formal education. She did, however, have an intense interest in medicine and anatomy. Volunteering to work at a hospital in New South Wales, she developed nursing capabilities, although she was not a registered nurse. Working under a surgeon, when she first encountered polio she was unsure how to treat the patients. With the recommendation of the surgeon, she decided to use heat as a pain-relieving measure. Dry heat and linseed wrappings did not provide comfort, so Kenny's next move was to lay strips of hot moist cloth over the affected areas, which reduced pain in some patients. This was the basis for what became known as the Kenny method, which later included physical therapy such as bending and flexing the joints for rehabilitation.[186]

In 1940, Kenny was able to travel to the United States to seek endorsement for her methods and was given space at the Minneapolis General Hospital. While many doctors dismissed her work, others embraced her therapy.[187]

The Smith family adopted her methods. The old wringer was used to squeeze the water out of the moist cloth strips that were placed on Elaine's legs throughout the day and night. In the end, when Elaine recovered, she had an affected leg three inches shorter than the other leg.

During her recovery, the family endured six weeks of quarantine, and because they chose the Kenny method for treatment, they received no assistance from the state or federal government. The milk that was delivered in bottles in those days was poured into a pan left waiting for the milkman on the porch; groceries were ordered by phone from the Thompson Brothers store and were delivered and also left on the porch; as good neighbors do, Thompson Brothers allowed the family to run a tab for the groceries during this difficult period. The children were confined to their own yard, isolated from contact with other children. Elaine's books and supplies were burned at the local school as a precaution.

Her illness was followed by intensive physical therapy administered by a local masseuse, who exercised and stretched the leg. And even though bicycles were rationed during the war years, eventually Elaine received a much-prized bicycle to help with her recovery. In the end, through the physical therapy routine, her affected leg eventually took on a normal appearance and was even slightly longer than the other leg.

Nurses were required throughout the Wilds region. Four from McKean County had completed instruction in the Kenny treatment by August 1944. The McKean County Society for Crippled Children sent nurses to Pittsburgh hospitals to practice the use of the Kenny method.[188]

Eventually, the epidemic subsided with the advent of cold weather. By October 31, the state had declared that the emergency was over.

German Prisoners of War Held in the Allegheny National Forest

In an earlier chapter, it was noted that Civilian Conservation Corps camps were set aside, with many being located in the Pennsylvania Wilds region. As the country entered the war, the camps that had still been operating were closed or used in other ways—like to house conscientious objectors to perform work projects in place of military service. As time went on, the camps were soon used for another purpose: housing German prisoners of war.

More than one thousand Nazi prisoners were housed at Red Bridge, Bull Hill and Duhring Camps, where they were put to work cutting wood to help the United States with a critical shortage of pulp and chemical wood.[189] Eventually, the prisoners were used to construct roads and plant hundreds of thousands of trees as part of a reforestation program in the Allegheny National Forest.[190]

The first contingent of German POWs arrived at Bull Hill CCC camp near Sheffield on August 16, 1944. On November 18, 1944, others arrived at the Red Bridge Camp near Kane. Shortly after the November arrivals, Camp Duhring outside of Marienville was filled.[191]

When the early prisoners first arrived in the region, a local newspaper reported that they appeared "happy and carefree, singing their national anthem at the top of their voices as they passed through town."[192] As time went on, newer prisoners arriving at Camp Duhring located seventeen miles south of Kane, were unlike the previous arrivals. These new arrivals were silent, not speaking to one another as they passed through town. Witnesses at the unloading said that one of the prisoners appeared to be a boy no older than twelve. Overall, the group contained men of all ages and sizes.[193]

Unlike prisoners held by the Germans, these prisoners were given an opportunity to volunteer for work in the woods and were paid the usual rate of pay for prisoners, about eighty cents per week.[194] The prisoners ran their camps and ate the same army rations as the U.S. soldier guards watching over them. A physician made regular inspections, and infirmaries were maintained at the camps. Visiting chaplains conducted religious services. Prisoners were permitted three packs of cigarettes and three bottles of beer a week. Each prisoner was permitted to have a Swastika flag on a table near his bunk along with pictures from home. The prisoners were up at 5:30 a.m. to begin work at 7:00 a.m. They were given a lunch break at noon, with a meal being hauled from a kitchen overseen by a German assigned to KP. The prisoners were dressed warmly and taken to the worksite by Army transports.[195]

Two publications were allowed into camp, the *New York Times* and a German-language newspaper published in New York. The prisoners were allowed to hear war news over a radio, which, depending on the reports, caused their spirits to rise or fall.[196]

It appears that the prisoners respected the guards who were watching over them, knowing that many of the guards had already been overseas. The camps were surrounded by guard towers. The prisoners understood the word *halt* and knew that the guards meant business.[197] Search lights, barbed wire fencing and machine guns on the watchtowers were standard precautions.

Camp Duhring historic marker. *Andrew Myers.*

South corner of entrance triangle at Camp Duhring. *Library of Congress.*

German prisoners of war at Camp Duhring, with their status clearly marked on their backs. *Buehler family photo.*

While prison escapes were rare, some did happen. In July 1945, three POWs housed at Red Bridge placed dummies in their beds to fool the guards during inspection. They tramped through the woods for many miles, finally emerging on the highway above Kinzua. One was captured there and was made to walk back to Red Bridge, while the other two safely swam across the Allegheny River. Arriving at a coal mining region at Scandia, they were spotted by an oil lease worker, who reported them to the Warren police. The two were found walking along the road toward the main highway and promptly surrendered.

Another break occurred the next day from the Duhring Camp. Two men, dressed in dungarees and wearing blue fatigue jackets with "POW" painted on them, walked away while a soccer game was in progress.[198] They were both apprehended.

Another escape by two men in December 1945 involved Karl Heckel, one of the same men who had escaped from Duhring in July. Apprehended in Ridgway, Heckel slashed his wrist in a suicide attempt.[199]

In reading about the treatment of the German prisoners in accordance with the Geneva Convention, one can contrast the relatively good treatment they received compared to the treatment received by Clark Ingram, a U.S. prisoner of war, recounted later in this book.

The camps were closed shortly after the conclusion of the war. Ten years later, in 1955, a former German prisoner of war at Duhring returned to take a look at the camp. Gerhard Baum, who was confined at Duhring for a year after being captured in the African campaign, found no barbed wire enclosures or evidence of wartime. The camp buildings were being used for summer camp groups of youngsters swimming in Spring Creek and hiking through the pines planted by the original occupants of the camp, the CCC. Baum wanted to enter the United States directly years before but was unable to get into the country. Three years before returning to Duhring, he was admitted to Canada and then came into the United

States to work in Buffalo, thereby providing him with an opportunity to revisit the camp.[200]

An even more remarkable account of a German POW named Franz Wenisch, who returned to the area twice, in 1978 and again in 1993, was told in his own words in the pages of local newspapers, a story of friendship throughout those many years:

> *A short review of myself will help you to understand this story of friendship of over 30 years. I was draughted* [drafted] *to the German Army (Wehrmacht) in 1943 at the age of 18; was captured in Italy near Florenz in Sept., 1944. It was the first touch to American people—soldiers of the U.S. Army. My knowledge of the English language, picked up during attending a high school in Czechoslovakia—Stribo—a little town very close to Pilzen—where the very famous beer is from. My trust in God and finally my trust in people gave me a lot of occasions to know about America itself, the American people because I was interested in meeting people, their daily lives and their customs. The first days of prisonship in Italy were very hard—a lot of questioning was done and I was lucky indeed when an American officer let me know—"We like the trait, but we don't like a traitor, and you'll come to the USA soon." So it happened on the 14th of Nov., 1944, when I arrived on the H.M. Santa Ryeon from Neapel* [Naples], *Italy, after a 12-day travel in a convoy of about 6 boats, in New York City. A little bit sad I passed the Statue of Liberty as a POW. From then on I always kept in my mind to pass this place—reminding of freedom—at any time later; and this one of my dreams became true. Going on, I wish to tell about the life as a POW in your country....* [W]*e went up by train via Pittsburgh to Kane, called the "Ice-pole of PA." It was quite a comfortable journey. We got the first lunch packages, and one of the accompanying GI's told me how the future life may go on. I had some troubles to understand everything: my British accent language missed the word "truck" and I couldn't find out how we should be brought to work as busy wood-cutters—in the country of William Penn....The train stopped at Kane rail station and on Army trucks we were taken to our next stay—nobody knew for how long—the POW Camp at Marienville. Here I lived with 250 prisoners surrounded by a wire fence, guarded by GI's for nearly 20 months. I met a lot of people, people of different behaviors under stress situations, but my believing in the goodness of human beings made my stay as a POW easier than I've thought before. I tried to be busy in improving my English, helped other POW's learning the language, and*

Top: "Big Boss" Otto Buehler (*far right, front row*) with prisoners of war at Camp Duhring, along with a guard and one of his children. *Buehler family photo.*

Bottom: Otto Buehler demonstrates tree cutting. *Buehler family photo.*

> *last not least, I got a promotion as a "supervisor" and within this new job I met the Buehler family from Ridgway. First of all our so called "Big Boss"—Otto Buehler, a PA wood-contractor. He was a great and a very good man indeed—God bless his soul.*[201]

Otto Buehler was born in Spring Creek Township, Elk County, Pennsylvania, in 1906. His mother and father, Anna Brawand Buehler and Fred Buehler, were immigrants from Switzerland. They were the parents of a large, enterprising family, with the 1910 census, the first taken after the birth of Otto, revealing nine children in the household at that time.

By 1940, when the U.S. government required registration for the draft, Otto was married to the former Edythe Anderson, still living in Elk County, and he was the father of four children, his family eventually growing to eight living children. His draft registration described him as five-foot-eleven, with a ruddy complexion, black hair and brown eyes.

With his parents' native language having been Schweizer Deutsch, one can assume that Otto spoke some German and understood it as well. His association with the wood industry as a contractor for the Armstrong Forest Company, a division of the New York and Pennsylvania Company that operated a paper mill in Johnsonburg and managed thousands of acres of woodlands in Pennsylvania, contributed to him supervising the German prisoners of war at Camp Duhring in Marienville, including Franz Wenisch and the men who surrounded him.

Wenisch continued to describe what became a friendship that lasted for years:

> *Later I met some of his children, especially the twins, and finally his nice, kindly and helpful wife, Edythe. They all demonstrated a real friendship, helped where they could, and began a very good fraternization directly in their home country. I only can underline I met so many nice people here, I couldn't forget to thank them and this in the name of the whole group who worked with Otto Buehler.*[202]
>
> *Otto was so good to us. When the food got bad, he brought in what he could. He helped when and where he could, and always treated us fairly. I never forgot that.*
>
> *The day I left the States, my family was forced to flee Czechoslovakia. It took me 11 days to find them once I got back to Germany.*[203]

Franz Wenisch, a German POW who formed a long-lasting friendship with the Buehler family. *Buehler family photo.*

Wenisch spent years rebuilding his life by becoming a teacher and a headmaster. But through the years, he never forgot the kindness of the American family who befriended him. On his first trip in 1978, he spent time with the Buehler family, although Otto, the "Big Boss," had passed in 1968. On his second trip in 1993, he spent several days with Otto's eldest son, James Buehler, and was in Ridgway to celebrate the eightieth birthday of Otto's wife, Edythe.

On this last visit, Wenisch stopped by the former POW camp at Marienville and recalled many events that took place there. He pointed out an area in the camp where Otto would pick them up each morning for their work in the forest, which was also the spot where the prisoners lined up for the last time before being returned to their home country.

As Wenisch was being driven away from the camp by Jim Buehler, he said that he didn't think he would be coming back to the camp again. "I really don't think I need to. The camp isn't the thing that draws me here anymore. We have the Buehler family and their friendship, which has lasted for 50 years. That's the important thing, and the thing I am thankful for."[204]

As time went on, several of Otto's family members visited Wenisch at his home in Germany, and the friendship lasted until Wenisch passed away several years ago.

Part V

WAR HEROES

Many of the small towns throughout the Wilds participate in a program known as Hometown Heroes, where photos of servicemen are displayed on banners attached to light posts through the main part of the town. The following are the names and stories of a few hometown heroes, who may or may not be recognized in a formal Hometown Heroes program, but nevertheless, they were ordinary people who were called on for extraordinary duty. Their stories illustrate the grit and determination of the Greatest Generation. Some of the people were known to the author personally. Others were located through the pages of newspapers and by filling in the details of their lives through sites such as Ancestry.com, where their war records are visible.

Wilfred "Bud" Neubert, hometown hero banner in Brockway, Pennsylvania. *Brianne Fleming and the* Tri-County Weekend, *November 9–10, 2024.*

One hometown hero from St. Marys in Elk County, who passed away in 2017 at the age of ninety-five, had been a prisoner of war, captured by the Germans after parachuting out over Normandy on D-Day. Speaking about his experiences when he was ninety-two years old, Jack Kestler recounted his training as a parachuter for D-Day, noting that before the plane took off at 11:50 p.m. on June 5 to make the jump into Normandy, the general reminded them that they were well trained and expendable: "I didn't know what expendable meant, but I found out that it meant that there's a good chance you're not coming back out. It's funny the things that go through your mind at a time like that. Instead of being scared, I remember thinking—we're going to make the papers at home in the morning."[205]

Bill Jackson

> *Wilbur J. Jackson, husband of the former Grace McNair of Ridgway, is reported "missing" pending further investigation according to word received by Mrs. Jackson from the Navy Department at Washington. Jackson, a chief electrician's mate in the U.S. Navy, was performing his duty in the Manila Bay area when that section fell into Japanese hands. The Navy Department has no report of his death or injury, and Jackson may be a prisoner of war. It will probably be several months before definite information can be expected. Mrs. Jackson and daughter reside on Depot Street.*
>
> —*"In a Paragraph,"* Kane (PA) Republican, *June 5, 1942*

The 1930 census reveals seventeen-year-old Grace McNair living on Depot Street in Ridgway, the county seat of Elk County, with her family: her father, William, listed as a valuation engineer in the oil and gas industry; her nineteen-year-old sister, Marion; her brother William, twelve years old; and her sister Virginia, eight years old. A delayed birth certificate filed in 1954 listed her mother as Mabel Gertrude Griffith of Somerville, Massachusetts, who had apparently passed by 1930. The birth certificate reveals that Grace was born in Erie County, Pennsylvania, in 1913. Her father's line of work took them to many locations, and in the 1920 census, the family residing in Chautauqua, New York. Grace came to consider Ridgway her hometown and had a wide circle of friends living there.

Research has not produced a lot of information on Grace during the ten years between the federal census in 1930 and 1940 except that she was still in Elk County in 1935. Somehow she made her way to Kittery, Maine, where on September 30, 1938, she married Wilbur Joseph Jackson.

Jackson, known to his friends as Bill, was born in Iowa in 1913. In the 1920 census, the family were living in South Dakota, where his father's occupation was farm manager. By 1930, the family were living in Detroit, where his father was a machinist in an auto factory and Bill was a student. By the 1940 census, the young married couple were residing in San Diego, California, where Bill was listed as an electrician in the U.S. Navy.

In an article about modern-day navy strategies, its author, Lieutenant Commander Joel Howitt, in October 2017 recalled navy history between World War I and II and the lessons that were learned. In those years, the navy generated a war plan that was codenamed Orange. The plan assumed that the Japanese would start a war without warning, taking the Philippines, which they did. Plan Orange called for a massive build-up of U.S. forces and an island-hopping campaign that would eventually reach Japan and defeat its forces.[206]

One can speculate how wide-spread the plan was known among the navy's enlisted men. Bill Jackson, possibly through participation in war gaming for Plan Orange or because of news regarding the Japanese, had the presence of mind to send his wife, Grace, home to Ridgway shortly before Pearl Harbor was bombed. In December 1941, he was serving as chief electrician's mate assigned to the USS *Canopus* (AS-9), Submarine Squadron 20.[207]

The USS *Canopus* had an interesting history. It was launched in 1919 as the *Santa Leonora* by New York Shipbuilding Company, Camden, New Jersey, and was acquired by the navy in 1921. The ship was converted to a submarine tender and renamed *Canopus*, designated as AS-9. Originally assigned to the Atlantic Fleet Submarine Force, by 1923 it was in San Pedro, California.

USS *Canopus* (AS-9) with the Asiatic Fleet Submarine Squadron. *Wikimedia Commons*.

Eventually sailing to Pearl Harbor, *Canopus* tended Submarine Division 17 of the Battle Force and sailed for permanent duty with the U.S. Asiatic Fleet in September 1924. The ship began a regular schedule of services in Manila Bay in 1924 and each summer was based with the fleet at Tsingtao, China. Between 1927 and 1931, the *Canopus* was flagship of submarine divisions, Asiatic Fleet. The ship was later assigned to Submarine Division 10 and was flagship of Submarine Squadron.[208]

On December 7, 1941, *Canopus* was at the Cavite Navy Yard south of the city of Manila as tender to Submarine Squadron 20. One can imagine the state of readiness that kept the men busy after the attack on Pearl Harbor. Daily air raids caused damage to ships, and the crew worked day and night to keep the submarines assigned to them at sea. When the army fell back on Manila, the ship sailed to the tip of Bataan to a site known as Mariveles Bay on Christmas Day 1941. The ship received direct bomb hits on December 29, 1941, and again on January 1, 1942. The ship received substantial damage injuring thirteen of its men. To prevent further attacks, smoke pots were placed around the ship during the daytime to give the appearance of an abandoned ship while working on repairs under cover of night. By the New Year, the last of the submarines had left *Canopus*. The activity then turned to caring for small craft and equipment for the army and navy. The ship's men even went into battle as a naval battalion on Bataan. With the surrender of Bataan in April 9, 1942, the ship was ordered to be scuttled and sunk.[209]

The Americans fought valiantly but eventually were overrun by the Japanese. Bataan surrendered on April 9 and Corregidor on May 6, 1942.

Bill Jackson was on one of those submarines that left the USS *Canopus* just before the new year of 1942. Through his own testimony, it is known that his submarine was hit by a Japanese torpedo, and he was picked up by a Japanese "hell ship." Taken to a location where there were other POWs, Jackson endured the Bataan Death March, eventually being housed in Bilibid Prisoner of War Camp located near Manila.

An excellent report, "American Prisoners of War in the Philippines—Office of the Provost Marshal General Report, November 19, 1945," describes conditions suffered by the prisoners. The Imperial Japanese Army demanded that Corregidor surrender when Bataan surrendered, and if not, any of those captured later would not be treated as prisoners of war but as captives. And as Corregidor did not immediately surrender, those taken prisoner were subjected to more ruthless treatment than was experienced by any other group of prisoners in the Philippines. With complete disregard to international law, they attempted to humiliate and degrade the Americans in the eyes of the Philippine people.

Most of the Bataan prisoners were made to go on forced marches a distance of 140 miles from where they had been captured. The Japanese made no attempt to supply transportation, food or water and carried out beatings and executions throughout the march.[210]

Later, when General Wainwright agreed to the unconditional surrender of Corregidor and eventually all U.S. forces in the Philippines, about eight thousand American soldiers, sailors and marines, along with five thousand Filipino troops and civilians, were taken captive by the Japanese. They were forced to march through Manila to show that the Japanese were superior to the White men. After the march, the prisoners arrived at Bilibid prison. At that time, although the prison was holding about twelve thousand prisoners, it was designed for four thousand at most. Every day, large groups of the prisoners were evacuated to Cabanatuan prison camp in northern Luzon.[211]

Bilibid was a former civilian prison converted to a POW camp, hospital and transit camp for POWs. Almost every man captured on Corregidor passed through this camp on their way to other camps. Hell ship survivors passed through the infamous prison, and more than 80 percent of the Bataan Death March survivors passed through this camp.[212]

Bill Jackson arrived at Bilibid prison with a leg wound. Seeing what was taking place and fearing that should his wound heal he would be transferred farther into the interior as so many others had been, he kept the leg wound open in an effort to save himself. The horrors and inhumane conditions that he and so many others experienced never left the memories of the survivors. The prisoners received bad treatment, in part because they couldn't understand the Japanese language and frequently were punished due to unintentional disobedience to orders that they simply didn't understand. The local Japanese commanders were also indifferent to the treatment of the prisoners and inflicted mistreatment as a matter of revenge:[213]

> *The Navy Department announced today the names of 41 Pennsylvanians, including a woman lieutenant in the nurse corps, who are held as prisoners of war by the Japanese, mostly in the Philippine islands. In each case the next of kin has been notified. The names are included in a list of 1,044 made public by the Navy and brings to 2,304 the total confirmed prisoners of war affecting the personnel of the naval services. The Pennsylvanians and next of kin include, Gustafson, Wilbert Theodore, painter first class—mother, Mrs. Clara Gustafson, 311 E. 25th Street, Erie; Jackson, Wilbur*

Joseph, chief electricians mate—wife, Mrs. Grace Veronica Jackson, 114 Depot Street, Ridgway; Price, William Joseph, torpedoman third class—mother, Mrs. Gladys Elizabeth Jordan, 178 W. Washington Street, Bradford; Williams, Robert Lee, seaman first class—father, Mr. Theo. Paul Williams, 206 West Church Street, Cory.[214]

A tall muscular man at the time of his captivity, after three years in Bilibid prison Jackson was emaciated when he was liberated. His own words were expressed in a local newspaper in 1945:

"I still can't believe it," said Wilbur Jackson when he arrived in Ridgway Wednesday to visit his wife and family, the former Grace McNair of that place, after spending three years in a Japanese prison in Manila. Jackson, a Chief Electrician's Mate, was in the U.S. Submarine service and stationed in Manila when Pearl Harbor was attached. He was seized by the Japs when Corregidor fell. In reference to treatment during his long internship, Jackson said the food was not very good; the internees were forced to work hard, building roads, etc., and many of the prisoners died. He weighed 100 pounds when liberated on Feb. 4. Today his weight is 189 pounds.[215]

Bill Jackson made a career of the navy, serving twenty-four years. He attained the rank of lieutenant, which is equivalent to the rank of captain in the army. He spent around forty-five years as a resident of San Diego, but Ridgway and the Pennsylvania Wilds was a special place for him where he and his family visited over the years. In his obituary from January 23, 2000, it noted that he was a member of the Elks Lodge of Ridgway.[216]

John North

Jefferson Barracks, Missouri, February 14, 1943:

Dear Ann, Howard & Family—How is everyone? I don't get time to write very much, that is why I haven't written before. We hardly get any time to sleep, they keep us so busy. I suppose you know I was drafted on the 15th of January. Well I did manage to get in the air forces.

This is just a basic training camp. We only get 26 days of basic training. I have had 15 days already. The boys that have had experience in some line of work that they need in the air corps are given exams to see if they can qualify for further training in that line. I was classified as an automobile mechanic. They told me that after I finished here I would be sent to a school for advanced automobile mechanics. Or if there wasn't an opening in that I would be sent to a school on instrument repair work.

I was on K.P. once since I have been here from 3:30 o'clock in the morning until 9 o'clock at night. You take turns on K.P., everyone has it at least once while they are here.

Missouri is an awful state. There isn't a hill anyplace. And the weather, one day you freeze and the next day you roast. Today it was about 15 degrees above zero, the other day it was 80 degrees above zero. We drill six days a week whether it is cold or not. You just stay out in it till you get so cold you can't even move. We sleep in tents, there is six men to a tent. I was lucky enough to get in a tent that don't leak. Some of them leak so much that every time it rains, everyone in it gets soaked.

We do get good meals here. We get ice cream once a day, sometimes twice a day. And we get pie once a day.

One thing I don't like is crawling out in a cold tent every morning at 5 o'clock. They even make us get up that early on Sunday. I will write again as soon as I get time. With love, Johnny

Letter sent to Ann and Howard Myers, aunt and uncle, Ridgway, PA[217]

This letter reveals that John North was a thoughtful young man in reaching out to his aunt and uncle about his recent experiences in the military.

John North was born in DuBois, Clearfield County, in 1923, the son of James and Bessie Minns North. He was the second child in a family of five children, the eldest of three sons.

His maternal great-grandparents, George and Alice Hunter Minns, emigrated from England in 1869. In 1879, the growing family came to the DuBois area, settling outside the city in a location known locally as Clear Run. George Minns worked for John DuBois Jr., founder of the city of DuBois, opening mines for Mr. DuBois. A self-made man, eventually he operated two mines on leased coal lands and supplied the tanneries at DuBois and Falls Creek. Minns won a contract to construct a water tunnel for John E. DuBois, successor of John DuBois Jr., through the Juniata Summit, connecting with the DuBois city system, a distance of 1,542 feet, bringing a good supply of water into town.

North's maternal grandfather, John T. Minns, was also a contractor and owner of Minns Coal Company and was well known in the DuBois region.

A review of DuBois High School yearbooks reveals that North was a member of student council. Alongside his graduation photo in 1941, it's noted that his course work included the machine shop, and by 1942, John was working as an attendant at McGarvey Motor Sales on West Washington Avenue in DuBois.

John was drafted on January 15, 1943. His draft card described him as six-foot-one in height and 160 pounds, with light complexion, brown hair and blue eyes.

As expressed in his letter to his aunt and uncle, he became an assistant aerial engineer, serving with the 22nd Bombardment Group, known as the Red Raiders. He attained the rank of staff sergeant and served in the Pacific, based on Owi Island.[218]

Owi Airfield was built under orders of General Douglas MacArthur. Spanning nearly the entire length of Owi Island, it was located in what

Second Lieutenant John H. Shear crew, circa 1943. John North is in the back row, second from the right. *Fold3.*

is today known as Biak Numfor Regency or Papua Province in Indonesia. The island was secured by the U.S. Army's 41st Infantry Division, 163rd Infantry Regiment, Company A, on June 2, 1944, and U.S. Army engineers arrived on June 3, 1944. The U.S. Army's 864th Engineer Aviation Battalion, Company B, began construction on June 8, 1944. By June 17, 1944, enough of the runway had been completed so that some P-38 Lightning planes from the 8th Fighter Group, 36th Fighter Squadron, from Wake Airfield were able to land on the partially completed runway during bad weather. The airfield was completed in three weeks.[219]

The 22nd Bombardment Group, to which North was assigned, was established in December 1939. In 1942, it was moved to the Southwest Pacific, where it attacked enemy shipping, installations and airfields. In February 1944, it was equipped with B-24s and began bombing Japanese airfields and shipping. In September 1944, it began attacking the southern Philippines in preparation for the invasion of Leyte.[220]

On October 14, 1944, John North and crew left Owi Island in their B-24 aircraft on a mission to strike Balikpapan, Borneo. Over the coast of Borneo, the B-24s in the strike group were attacked by enemy fighter planes using phosphorus bombs. An eyewitness report noted that the formation was intercepted by ten to fifteen fighters that dropped these bombs. The plane John was in, no. 992, was hit by a phosphorus bomb or anti-aircraft fire and dropped away from formation with two engines smoking. The plane was seen losing altitude rapidly, and five to seven men bailed out. Immediately after the men exited the plane, it went into a straight vertical dive down to the water.[221] The crew were captured and imprisoned.

Conditions in the war camps were brutal. One account is recorded of a Japanese captain who was over the Sandakan Camp in northern Borneo telling newly arrived POWs, "You will work until your bones rot under the tropical sun of Borneo. You will work for the Emperor. If any of you escape, I will pick out three or four and shoot them. The war will last for 100 years."[222]

In May 1945, after Sandakan airfield had been under heavy bombing by Allied forces, the Japanese closed the airfield and the camp which was close by. The commander of the camp ordered 536 prisoners to march to Ranau. He then ordered the camp to be set on fire, which also destroyed all the records. Other prisoners from Sandakan were marched into the jungle, where they died or were shot by Japanese guards. By June 10, 1945, another 30 prisoners had died, and a final march of 75 prisoners toward Ranau took place. Prisoners who were stranded near the burned-out area of the former camp either died of malnutrition and disease or were killed by Japanese guards. By August 15, 1945, none of the prisoners who was marched from the Sandakan camp remained alive.[223]

On July 3, 1945, Balikpapan was liberated. Sadly, with liberation at hand, John North and others with him were executed by their Japanese captors, who were trying to save themselves.[224] He was buried in a mass grave with seven other POWs. In 1950, his body and the bodies of those buried with him were returned to Jefferson Barracks, Missouri, where they rest in a mass grave together. John North was never again to see the hills of the Pennsylvania Wilds that were so familiar to him.

James Litherland

There was a popular World War II song made famous by British singer Vera Lynn titled "The White Cliffs of Dover." The words were written by an American who had never visited the UK and apparently didn't know that there are no bluebirds as we in the states know them in England. Those lyrics illustrate the hope of the British people for peace: "There'll be bluebirds over the White Cliffs of Dover, tomorrow, just you wait and see…there'll be love and laughter and peace ever after, tomorrow, when the world is free." There has been some speculation that the lyricist was not

White Cliffs of Dover. *John Myers.*

writing about the nonexistent bluebirds in the sky over the White Cliffs, but rather was referring to the U.S. airmen flying their planes across Dover on their way to Europe and returning on that same route. Let's speculate that the song did apply to the U.S. fliers, and James Litherland, born and raised in the Pennsylvania Wilds, was most certainly one of those "bluebirds."

> *Welcome home dear brother, you are not forgotten.*[225]

These words were spoken by Captain Matt Lower, an army chaplain at Fort Dix, New Jersey, at a September 2023 ceremony to honor and bury Second Lieutenant James Litherland III, who had been declared missing in action on February 28, 1944, when the plane he was on went down near the city of Le Translay, France. Three of the airmen on board successfully parachuted out, while seven other crew members, including Litherland, were still on board.[226]

A March 1944 newspaper clipping provided additional information about the lieutenant:

> *Lieut. Litherland Missing Over France*
> *Official word was received from the War Department yesterday that Second Lieut. James Litherland of South Williamsport, is missing in action over France.*
>
> *His family was notified yesterday that the young officer, a co-pilot on a Flying Fortress, failed to return from a bombing mission of Feb. 28—the day upon which his only child, Suzanne, was born in the Williamsport Hospital.*
>
> *On 11 Missions*
> *He had completed 11 missions early in February and had been awarded the Army Air Medal with oak leaf clusters for his exploits.*
>
> *Lieutenant Litherland is the son of Mrs. James Litherland, 2nd of 15 West Seventh Avenue, South Williamsport. His wife, the former Miss Wilma Jane Wurster, daughter of Mrs. William F. Wurster, resides with her mother at 328 Lowe Street, South Side.*[227]

Litherland was born November 22, 1918, in South Williamsport. He registered for the draft on October 16, 1940, and at the time was working for Jones & Laughlin Steel Corporation. His registration reveals that he was five-foot-eight and weighed 130 pounds. He had a light complexion,

The 303rd Bombardment Group, Neil Shoup Company. Neil Shoup, pilot, and James Litherland, copilot (*back row, right*). *Fold3*.

brown hair and blue eyes. In the 1930 census, the Litherland family consisted of James Litherland Jr., head of household; Elizabeth, his wife; son James, eleven; daughter Avid Anne, seven; and mother-in-law, Edith Schneider. His father died in 1936, and in the 1940 census, James was living at home with his mother, sister and grandmother.

James enlisted in the U.S. Army Air Corps in 1942 as an aviation cadet. While he was in training in South Dakota in 1943, he married Wilma Jane Wurster, who was also from Williamsport. In 1942, the Rapid City Army Base, later known as Ellsworth Air Force Base, was opened to train B-17 Flying Fortress heavy bomber units to fight in Europe.[228] In November 1943, he was deployed to Molesworth Airbase in England and assigned to the 359th Bomber Group.[229]

Molesworth is an ancient village located in Cambridgeshire. It was recorded in the Domesday Book during a survey carried out at the order of William the Conqueror in 1085.

During the First World War, the Royal Flying Corps chose a site near the village of Old Weston for an airfield. Old Weston is near Molesworth. At the start of World War II, the Royal Air Force selected the area for a site that would become RAF Molesworth. The airfield was built between 1940 and 1941. The site was briefly used by the Royal Australian Air Force 460 Squadron and the RAF Bomber Command 159 Squadron. In February 1942, the site was inspected by Americans for possible use by the air force. Improving the facility during 1942 to a Class A airfield, all of its runways were extended to American specifications for heavy four-engine bombers. The first U.S. Air Force group at Molesworth was the 15th Bombardment Squadron, arriving on June 9, 1942.[230]

Litherland was assigned to the 303rd Bombardment Group, serving as copilot under Neil Shoup, captain and pilot. The plane they flew was dubbed the "Knockout Dropper."[231] Flying many combat missions, the B-17 Flying Fortress they were piloting was shot down by anti-aircraft fire after a bombing raid on a German V-2 rocket site in Blois-Coquerel, France. It is known that before the plane crashed, three airmen parachuted successfully. Litherland and seven other crew members were still on board when the plane crashed near Le Translay, France. Litherland's remains were never recovered.[232]

Reviewing German documents in 1945 that detailed American planes and their crews during the war reveals that six sets of remains were recovered near the crash site near Le Translay and were buried at the English World War I Memorial Cemetery in Abbeville, France, in March 1944. In June 1945, an American Graves Registration team located the six sets of remains and reinterred them at the U.S. Military Cemetery in St. Andre, France. Five of the six sets of remains recovered were identified. One unknown set was designated as "X-452 Andre." In March 1947, American Graves Registration Command investigators transferred the X-452 remains to the Suresnes American Cemetery, France. Litherland was officially declared non-recoverable on December 26, 1950.[233]

Litherland's name was recorded on the Tablets of the Missing at Ardennes American Cemetery in Neupre, Belgium. Over the years, investigators were unable to identify Litherland, although there was some association between X-452 and Litherland. In September 2017, an investigative team traveled to Le Translay to locate the crash site. In August 2018, evidence and remains were recovered from the site that were sent to a laboratory for analysis. In October 2019, the unknown remains designated "X-452 Andre" were exhumed from Suresnes American Cemetery.[234]

Using dental and anthropological analysis, along with mtDNA and autosomal DNA, the Defense POW/MIA Accounting Agency was able to identify Litherland's remains.

After seventy-nine years, James Litherland was finally returned to his hometown of Williamsport, where he was buried at Wildwood Cemetery next to his father and grandfather. His daughter, who only knew her father through photographs, noted that she had the opportunity to have him buried in France but stated, "I wanted him to be with his family."[235]

Litherland was honored with a twenty-one-gun salute by a military honor guard and the playing of taps. Captain Lower spoke to the forty family members and relatives who attended the private funeral, saying, "He died doing what he loved—serving America."[236]

William J. Price

William Joseph Price, better known to followers of Bradford High School athletic teams as "Heinie" who is a prisoner of the Japanese government and is located at Osaka camp in Japan, recently broadcast a message to his mother, Mrs. Gladys Manry, 196 Barbour Street extension.

The message, which was relayed to Mrs. Manry from Washington was intercepted as follows:

Mrs. Gladys Manry
196 Barbour street extension

The following enemy propaganda from the Japanese government has been intercepted, "I am in fair health. Sure will be a big explosion in the food line, tell everyone hello. Be sure Johnny Nelson of the—hears of this. Hope you are doing O.K. I suppose all the rest are gone by now. I Mean Murphy and Chuck. You and I may, if possible, do a little traveling when I get home. I received your package and was sure pleased. I suppose grandmother and the rest wonder how I am. I bet there are a lot of new songs in swing. I have lost my wanderlust feeling and have inducted myself in more ways than one. Send C. B. Miller, Tolleson, Arizona, Route One, Box 924 and tell his mother he is OK. Also insurance up to date.

Torpedoman 3rd Class
William Joseph Price
USN Osaka Camp[237]

William Price's story has been gleaned from the pages of the *Bradford Evening Star/Bradford Daily Record*. He was a popular student in high school, where he excelled in sports, and the newspaper reported in May 1942 that he was "the first casualty of a Bradford youth in foreign service with the armed forces of his country."[238] His mother received notice from the Navy Department in Washington that he was in Manila Bay in the Philippines when it capitulated to Japanese forces. The Navy Department noted that it would continue to carry him in its records, as it had no report of his death or injury; he might have been a prisoner of war.

The newspaper article noted that Price was a graduate of Bradford High School, class of 1937, and enlisted in the navy on October 8, 1940. He was sent to submarine school at New Haven, Connecticut, for his training and was later transferred to Pearl Harbor. A letter mailed from Pearl Harbor in November 1941 was the last word his family received. The article noted that his brother, Richard, twenty-one, had enlisted in the navy in September 1940 and was on duty in the Atlantic.[239]

By January 1945, his mother had received word that her son, William, was transferred from the Philippine Islands to a prison camp in Japan and that he had been a prisoner of the Japanese government since the fall of Manila, when he was taken prisoner.[240] He was assigned to a prisoner of war camp located at Osaka, Japan.

A description of some of the quarters used to house the prisoners of war is found in "History of the Oaka Main Camp-Chikko." It had two one-story barracks, each seventy-two by thirty-three feet, with triple-decker bunks. A third building, seventy-two by thirty feet, was also of two-story construction, with a space on the first floor, thirty by twenty-four feet, used as a sick ward; the second floor contained the POW quarters. A fourth building, sixty-four by thirty feet, held prisoners on the second floor only. Also described was a kitchen, thirty feet square, with eight brick stoves, and a cement bath ten feet square with ten showers. The dispensary was a room twenty-one feet square housed next to the guard house and containing one cell.

The Osaka camp was established to provide workers for the docks and stevedoring companies at Osaka port. The prisoners wore their own clothing along with Japanese uniforms. Their shoes were either their own or Japanese army shoes.

The food was simple: breakfast was rice and soup; lunch was rice with sometimes bread and seaweed; dinner included rice and soup, fish every ten days, meat once or twice a month and vegetables, such as onions or potatoes.[241]

According to some who investigated the treatment of prisoners of war by the Japanese, the POWs were subjected to severe brutality, hard labor, disease, starvation and humiliation. Others explain that the high mortality rates and horrid conditions among the POWs was due to logistical difficulties, inattention and poor planning in running the camps.[242] Their disdain for those captured and their treatment of prisoners were attributed to a Japanese culture of non-surrender.

W.J. Price, 27,
Home After 4 Years Prison

Former Bradford High Basketball Star captured by Japs in Dec. 1941

"Hello, Mom, here I come" was a phrase that brought tears of happiness to Mrs. Francis Manry of Barbour St. Ext. yesterday when she received

> *the telegram from a son, William J. (Heinie) Price, torpedoman, 3c, U.S. Navy, who had been a prisoner of the war of the Japanese government since the attack on Pearl Harbor.*
>
> *The wire was dispatched from Omaha, Neb. Stating that Price would be in Chicago Tuesday and in Salamanca at 5 a.m. today. Mrs. Manry went to Salamanca this morning to greet her son, who she hadn't seen since he enlisted Oct. 8, 1940.*[243]

Price was discharged from service on December 20, 1946, with the rank of chief petty officer. In December 1951, Price married Mary Jane Grandin, a 1944 graduate of Bradford High School. Mary Jane served in the U.S. Navy as a hospital corpsman during the Korean War from December 4, 1950, to April 8, 1952.[244]

Clark Ingram

Clark Ingram was well known throughout Bennetts Valley, having been born in Caledonia, Jay Township, Elk County, in 1921. The son of George R. Ingram and Hannah Anderson Ingram, he spent his young life in "the Valley" and graduated from Weedville High School in 1939.[245]

In the postwar years, he worked as a miner for a coal company; owned and operated trucks, a country store, a beef cattle farm and school buses; and was a strip mine owner. But not many people may have known that he was a German prisoner of war for twenty-three months or that he was credited with downing three enemy planes. He was decorated with the Air Medal, POW Medal, the Purple Heart, a Presidential Citation, the EAME (European–African–Middle Eastern) campaign ribbon with four stars and a Distinguished Unit Citation.[246]

Through the efforts of his granddaughter, the story of his service and captivity has been recorded for posterity. In a book titled *Clark Ingram, Prisoner of War*, Leigh Ingram O'Brien related the story of her grandfather's captivity by the Germans and his survival from Stalag Luft 6 and 4 (*luft* in German means "air"), whose prisoners were forced on a freezing and cruel death march that has been recorded in history as the infamous "Shoe Leather Express."

His draft card shows that he registered for the draft on February 16, 1942, at Caledonia. At the time, he was five-foot-eleven and weighed 175 pounds. His complexion was listed as "light," and he had blonde hair and blue eyes.[247]

Ingram enlisted in the U.S. Army Air Force in September 1942. Within his first year of service, he trained as a B17 radio operator. Making his way through various assignments, he was eventually assigned to the 345th Bomber Squadron at Benina Airfield, Benghazi, Libya, in 1943. His rank at the time was staff sergeant.[248]

Ingram served in four campaigns: Air Offensive Europe, Sicily, Naples-Foggia and Ploesti. Then, on September 3, 1943, while on a mission to Sulmona, Italy, the B24 Clark was flying in was attacked by German fighters. After it was hit by flak, several crew members parachuted out. Six of the ten crewmen survived, including Clark. Captured by Italian police, he was turned over to the Germans.

A headline in a Pennsylvania newspaper carried the news:

> *PA Soldiers*
> *Missing in Six*
> *Fighting Areas*
>
> *Washington. Today—(AP)—Forty-seven Pennsylvanians are included in a listing of 574 soldiers missing in action on six fighting fronts, the War Department announced today.…Staff Sgt. Clark R. Ingram, Weedville.*[249]

Ingram eventually ended up in the German Stalag system as a prisoner of war. Identified as Stalag Luft 4 and 6, the camps were designated for airmen. While he was interned, the Germans began steps to move prisoners out of Stalag Luft 4 and 6 to other locations. Their decision was based in some part on the Russian winter offensive that began in early January 1945 at the front some two hundred miles northwest of Warsaw. However, by February 3, 1945, the front line of the war was forty miles south of Luft 4, causing the Germans to evacuate various prisoner of war camps.[250]

While the "Shoe Leather Express" is not as well known as the Bataan Death March, some survivors have written about their experiences. One such veteran, Joseph P. O'Donnell, authored *The Shoe Leather Express, February 6, 1945, to May 2, 1945, 86 Days*. In it, O'Donnell described the actions of the Germans as the Russians closed in:

> *On January 15, 1945, the sick and crippled Prisoners of War were shipped by 40 and 8 boxcars to various POW camps elsewhere in Germany. The remaining "so-called" healthy POWs departed at various intervals, not knowing our destination, direction or a definite time of arrival. The*

> *Germans told us they were evacuating us to a better camp, a three-to-four-day march. This particular march, "The Shoe Leather Express" lasted for 86 days and 600 miles of beatings, starvation, amputations, frostbite, frozen feet and hands, dirt, lice, filth, degradation, heat, thirst and death. Many of the Prisoners of War referred to the march as "The Death March" or "The Black March"....Little has been written or filmed about the hardships encountered on these forced marches or the hardships encountered on the 40 and 8 boxcar rides. To dwell on camp life would be superfluous; we were there, all 9,000 of us.*[251]

Ingram and other POWs were liberated on April 16 at 11:15 by British General Montgomery's 2nd Army. Ingram weighed about one hundred pounds at the time of his liberation.

Returning to civilian life and apparently not deterred by the horrific conditions he had endured during the Shoe Leather Express, Ingram married Eleanor Gallagher in July 1945. They went on to raise three sons. This hero lived a long life, passing away in May 2011 at the age of eighty-nine.

Francis X. Kennedy

> *Francis Kennedy Wounded in Italy*
>
> *Emporium—Staff Sgt. Francis Kennedy, 21, was wounded while fighting with the Fifth Army in northern Italy on Feb. 20 according to a War Department message to his parents, Mr. and Mrs. Sidney Kennedy, of Driftwood.*
>
> *Sergeant Kennedy enlisted Jan 1, 1943, and trained at Camp Halle* [Hale], *Colorado, as a ski trooper. Last January he was sent overseas and was in the 85th Mountain Infantry. He was a sophomore at the Pennsylvania State College at the time of his enlistment.*[252]

The 10th Mountain Division of the 85th Mountain Infantry "started out as an experiment to train skiers and climbers to fight in the most difficult, mountainous terrain in Europe. Some of the men who joined the division were skiers already, while others had never seen a ski in their lives."[253]

The training camp for this experiment was Camp Hale near Pando, Colorado. The men who were sent there lived in the mountains for weeks.

Left: Camp Hale, Colorado. *Wikimedia Commons.*

Opposite: Three 10th Mountain Division ski troopers above Camp Hale, 1944. *Wikimedia Commons.*

Their training included skiing, snowshoeing and rock climbing. Living at altitudes of up to 13,500 feet, the men learned cold-weather survival tactics such as keeping warm by building snow caves. Temperatures often dropped to twenty degrees below zero at night.[254]

Nothing was learned in searching the records for Francis Kennedy as to why he joined this particular group. The answer was found in an interview with his wife and daughter by the *Williamsport Sun-Gazette* in 2018. Born in St. Marys, Pennsylvania, on June 29, 1923, he lived with his parents in Driftwood, Cameron County, Pennsylvania. He was enrolled at the Forest School at Mount Alto Campus of Penn State University, where he attended classes for one year before joining the army in January 1943. Training at Camp Hale, he served with the 86th Mountain Infantry, as well as the 85th Mountain Infantry, 10th Mountain Division, in Italy.[255]

According to his wife, Kennedy had never gone skiing before he became a member of the U.S. Army's 10th Mountain Division. Noting that units such as the 10th Mountain Division were rare to nonexistent in the U.S. military, his daughter said, "They had to invent their own equipment." The soldiers dressed in all white to blend in with the snowy terrain. One of the famous people who served with the 10th Mountain Division was Bob Dole, who later became a U.S. senator.[256]

At the end of 1944, the 10th Division was deployed and began a series of assaults against the German army in the northern Apennine Mountains of Italy. One of its objectives, Mount Belvedere, was the highest mountain in the Apennines. Blocked by the Germans from taking that location for nearly six months, the 10th Division, in a nighttime operation, took Riva Ridge on February 18, 1945, which prevented the Germans from being able to surveil U.S. troops below. It was a risky endeavor, as the steep mountain was covered with snow and ice. With conditions so difficult, the Germans did not have

guard patrols in the area, as they believed that no one could scale the ridge. Silently, the soldiers of the 10th Division climbed to the top and secured Riva Ridge with few casualties.

The next day, with Mount Belvedere as its objective, the American soldiers were victorious, but not without a price. Of the thirteen thousand soldiers in the division, nearly one thousand died.[257] Francis Kennedy suffered a leg wound in the battle. His daughter said, "He was crawling down the mountain to get to medics when he got shot."[258]

For a period of time, Kennedy was listed as missing. In the end, he was hospitalized and returned to the States. For his service, Kennedy was awarded the Bronze Star, the European Theater of Operations Medal with two Battle Stars, the Combat Infantry Badge, the Victory Medal and the Good Conduct Medal.[259] His daughter said, "He was in the hospital and [General] Eisenhower actually handed him his medals.[260]

Discharged in 1946, Kennedy returned to Penn State University, pursuing a degree in forestry, graduating in 1949. He and his wife, Janenne, were married at St. Mark's Church in Driftwood, Pennsylvania, on August 7, 1950.[261]

Kennedy, a true outdoorsman, served as district forester for Lycoming County for a number of years. The Francis X. Kennedy Ski Trail, known as the FXK, a 4.6-mile loop located in Tiadaghton State Forest near Waterville, Pennsylvania, was named for him.

In 2022, Camp Hale was named a national monument. Built in 1942, the site was deactivated in 1965. While no original buildings remain, visitors can find traces of the camp in the outlines of old structures and the climbing rock where the soldiers trained. The site originally accommodated 226 barracks, 33 administration buildings, a 676-bed hospital, a veterinary hospital, a bakery, a field house, 5 churches, several theaters, 100 mess halls and more. The site housed about 15,000 people, including 14,000 soldiers and 240 women who served in the Women's Army Corps. German and Italian prisoners of war were also held at the camp.

Part VI

PEACE

V-E DAY

The D-Day invasion of France in 1944 marked the "beginning of the end" for Nazi Germany. As troops set foot in France, they pushed across Europe toward Germany. The fight was far from over, with one of the fiercest offensives being the Battle of the Bulge in the Ardennes National Forest, where the Allied forces halted a German drive into the Belgian towns of Liege and Namur. Taking place in mid-December, the Battle of the Bulge marked the last occasion when Germany was able to initiate a major offensive on any front.[262]

In January 1945, the Soviet army began an offensive on the eastern front with the ultimate goal of capturing Berlin. With the Allied forces having reached the western border of Germany in February 1945, they penetrated the Siegfried Line and reached the Rhine River at several points. As the Allied forces advanced into Germany from the west, the Soviet army began its final advance against Berlin on April 19, 1945. On April 26, American and Soviet forces reached the town of Torgau on the Elbe River, about seventy miles from Berlin. Hitler committed suicide on April 30, and Berlin surrendered to the Soviet soldiers on May 2. On May 7, the German High Command accepted the Allies' unconditional surrender terms, and a surrender ceremony was held on May 7 at General Eisenhower's headquarters in Reims, France, followed by another surrender ceremony to the Soviets in Berlin on May 8.[263]

V-E Day, Piccadilly, London, 1945. *Wikimedia Commons.*

The news of V-E Day was quietly welcomed throughout the Wilds region. Various communities held church services to give thanks for the news of the German surrender. But factories that had geared up for war continued to operate, as the war was still raging in the Pacific. Soldiers who had been serving in Europe would now be transferred to the Pacific to bring that phase of the war to a conclusion.

A May 9, 1945 letter sent to Mrs. Eva Passinger in Warren from her son, Private First Class Floyd J. Passinger, a former member of the *Times-Mirror* editorial staff, provided insight into the events of the day:

> *Former Times-Mirror Staff Member Writes of V-E Day*
> *Well, it's all over in this theater now. Beating the Nazis was a big order and it took five years and eight months to fulfill it, but the job has been done—but well.*
>
> *It's something to marvel at when you think about it. A host of nations, blended together with a mutual cause and coordination realized as never before. Under one Supreme Commander these nations battered down a power that would have them yield the precious possessions that make life worth living.*
>
> *They didn't yield, and the power exists no longer. May it never be again on this earth that evil forces will endeavor to take by force the rightful freedoms of mankind.*
>
> *The celebration, I suppose, still lingers at home as well as in the British Isles and throughout Europe where people can breathe a free breath without fear again today. I only hope that with all the prayers, toasts and frivolity that those who profit by this great accomplishment will realize and fully*

appreciate the cost of V-E Day. May God tonight be with the heroic troops who made this V-E Day possible by unselfishly sacrificing their lives to accomplish the task. I saw some of them fall. They wanted to live, too, but they died willingly that those who linger might live in peace. Oh, if only we can preserve it once the entire job is finished with the defeat of Japan.

There was some confusion here as to just when V-E Day was to be official. We were told on Monday that today would be THE day, but later Tuesday was announced as the end of hostilities over here. Regardless of which day it is, it is comforting to know that half the job we began five years ago has been accomplished….I've been knocking out citations all day long, drafting the copies for the official award, and it has been a big job. We're giving some awards to the Russians with whom we established contact recently and that in itself was a job as I wrestled with their names. No Johnsons in Russia, I guess, but every other guy is named Ivan.

Guess that winds up tonight's journal so I'll say Guten Abend and hang up the receiver. With love from your ETO correspondent. Goodnight. Floyd.[264]

Another soldier from Tioga County, Private Gordon Rose, wrote to his father shortly after V-E Day was declared, his letter appearing on the *Mansfield Advertiser* on June 6, 1945:

Dear Dad: How's everything? It's certainly been a comparatively long time since I last wrote, but then, too, so have many breath-taking big and important events taken place during that time. Yessiree! Especially long awaited and expected was the climax of the war—that for which we have all prayed, fought, suffered, and many died.

Here the news was received with an anti-climactic air, for during the week preceding cessation of hostilities there was little activity on our army front. On the eve of V-E Day wine was made available to us to be used in the celebration of our victory, but rest assured that nary a drop of it was used in an excessive manner—G.I's were never more sober. I believe all of us realized that such actions were inappropriate for such an occasion. Instead, prayer and thanks were offered in memoriam of those who contributed life itself to the ultimate materialization of our complete victory. We could do no less than offer our respects to those thousands, including buddies, who fell by our sides.

While "sweating out" as to how the division will now be used (S. Pacific—Army of Occupation—or what), we are experiencing a taste of something bordering on garrison routine—some drill, pressed O.D.'s, wearing of decorations, military courtesy, etc. However, I'm not kicking, for all the while we are participating thusly, progress is being made elsewhere—hard earned progress, the sweat and blood type.

For the past few days I have been working away from my company. There is so much work to be accomplished on individual service records, etc., that the C.O. sent me down to help the clerk out—so here I am!

After about three months of playing tag with and "Christianizing" Jerries, I didn't think I'd be able to acclimate myself so readily to "clerking" work. However, after the first day I found myself as well adapted to it and enjoying it as much as I did while at Camp Wolters, Texas.

Well, Dad, guess these lines will have to do for now. I'm feeling the best, though the heat is terrific over her. So long for now, Dad. Lots of love—Gordy.[265]

V-J Day

V-J Day, announcement. *Wikimedia Commons.*

On August 14, 1945, word was received that Japan had surrendered unconditionally to the Allies. The formal surrender took place aboard the USS *Missouri*, anchored in Tokyo Bay. Following the surrender of Nazi Germany a few months earlier, the surrender ended years of hostilities in the Pacific.[266]

On July 26, 1945, Allied leaders, through what is known as the Potsdam Declaration, called on Japan to surrender, reassuring that if it did, Japan would have a peaceful government, but if it chose not to surrender, it would face "prompt and utter destruction."[267] The Japanese government chose not to surrender, which led to the August 6 attack by the American B-29 known as *Enola Gay* dropping an atomic bomb on Hiroshima, killing more than seventy thousand people, destroying a five-square-mile section of the city. Three days later, a second atomic bomb was dropped on Nagasaki, killing another forty thousand Japanese people. Emperor Hirohito realized that to continue to fight would "not only result in the collapse and obliteration of the Japanese nation, but would also lead to the total extinction of human civilization."[268]

Part VII

WHEN THE LIGHTS GO ON AGAIN ALL OVER THE WORLD

A popular World War II song made famous in the United States by Vaughn Monroe spoke of the return to normalcy that people across the globe were looking forward to:

When the lights go on again all over the world
And the boys are home again all over the world
And rain or snow is all that may fall from the skies above
A kiss won't mean "goodbye" but "Hello to love."

When the lights go on again all over the world
And the ships will sail again all over the world
Then we'll have time for things like wedding rings and free hearts will sing
When the lights go on again all over the world.[269]

With the news of Japan's unconditional surrender sweeping the country, the citizens of the Wilds quickly reacted with celebrations breaking out. In Chandlers Valley in Warren County, the news was announced by the "ringing of bells, the barking of dogs and the bawling of kids."[270]

In the small town of Sykesville in Jefferson County, celebrations began as soon as President Truman announced the surrender at 7:00 p.m., coinciding with celebrations in England, Russia and China:

In Sykesville, as in every other hamlet, town and city in the Allied world, joy ran rampant, young and old alike let their feelings have full sway, and the citizenry threw care and worry to the four winds when news of the surrender became official. Liquor dispensing places, as well as all other business establishments closed their doors immediately and an evening and night of solemnity, revelry and joyousness was in order. Shortly after official word was received via radio in this place, a rather large crowd of persons, among them sorrowing relatives and friends of Sykesville lads who had paid the supreme sacrifice, gathered at the Main Street Honor Roll, and with the cooperation of the Kramer Community Band gave thanks to the Lord for His deliverance from the evil of aggression. Led by a color guard of American Legion members, the band rendered several selections, followed by a prayer by Rev. James Kelly, pastor of the local Methodist church, and the sounding of "Taps" by Joe Valentine, of the Kramer Band. After the brief ceremony, the crowd gathered near the Main and Park street intersection and an evening of fireworks, horn-blowing, fire sirens and parades got underway.

Members of both sexes, young and old, joined in numerous parades, acts and stunts that was in keeping with the occasion. Among the noteworthy examples of good-natured fun, and the overflowing joy that abounded, were: Joe Tramontana, his grass skirt, Chinese hat and his hula-hula impersonations, which created quite a bit of amusement among the spectators; the Ideal Shirt Company girls who led the parades; W.K. Smith's century-note display of "hoarded" fireworks; the hanging in effigy of "Tojo," and numerous other extemporaneous acts that kept the huge crowd milling around the streets long after midnight.[271]

Relieved parents and family members began to look forward to the day when their sons and daughters would return home to begin a life of normalcy once again. Paul Shaffer, a native of Reynoldsville in Jefferson County, was on board the *Alabama*, part of Admiral Halsey's U.S. Third Fleet, waiting for the peace arrangements off the coast of Japan, when he wrote to his mother:

Dear Mother: The war is almost over! I say "almost" because even though the Japs have said that they want to quit fighting, life for me goes on in the same old way—points or no points. It seems to be more difficult to stop a war than it is to start one. A few things have changed, among them a relaxation of censorship restrictions. Although we still have censorship, we are now permitted to tell "all"—or at least almost all.... So you can discuss the "Saga of the Able Alabama" over the backyard fence or send it to the local newspaper is you desire.[272]

In Potter County, Mr. and Mrs. Frank Niver received letters from their two sons serving in the Pacific. Specialist Second Class Cleon Niver noted that he was headed home and that his ship had been in the invasions of Iwo Jima and Okinawa. At the time of the surrender, they were at Leyte.

His brother, Private Lyall Niver, wrote from the island of Luzon in the Philippines. He said that he was in the Marshall Islands on V-J Day. He also told his parents that as he passed through Manila, ice cream cups were selling for one paso, or fifty cents USD,[273] certainly a sign of normalcy returning to the region.

A return to normal life also meant the termination of rationing by the end of 1945, with the exception of sugar, which was rationed until June 1947. At first, the end of rationing caused goods to be in short supply simply because of demand.

War Brides

Some may be unfamiliar with Operation Magic Carpet, which had been organized by the U.S. government in the winter of 1945, an undertaking to bring home millions of American military personnel by sea and air. More than 8 million men and women were scattered across fifty-five theaters of war, spanning four continents. "Home Alive by '45" was on the minds of millions in uniform. And while this was being undertaken, there was another movement underway, bringing home the sixty thousand to seventy thousand foreign women who were married to American servicemen during the war years, women known as "war brides."

While it may seem like a doable task to bring these women to the States to be with their husbands, the United States had a quota system, the National Origins Formula established by the Immigration Act of 1924. That act cut off entry for many immigrants from Europe and all immigrants from Asia.

The returning GIs brought pressure on the political leaders in Washington to strike down the Immigration Act. In 1943, the government passed the Magnuson Act, which allowed a small number of Chinese immigrants' legal entry into the country for the first time in sixty years in recognition of China's fight in the war against Japan. Two years later, government leadership, under insurmountable public opinion, established a pathway forward for GI brides and sweethearts and formally passed the "War Brides Act." Enacted on December 28, 1945, its purpose was "To expedite the admission to the

American boy meets British girl—love and romance on the homefront. Bournemouth, England, 1941. *Wikimedia Commons.*

United States of alien spouses and alien minor children of citizen members of the United States armed forces." This act exempted war brides and their dependents from the 1924 "Immigration Act."[274]

While the planners of Operation Magic Carpet were unable to bring all U.S. service personnel home by the end of 1945 due to the logistics and distances involved, the war brides and their families often waited months and years to arrive in the States. The first group of war brides was from Britain, due in some part to the close relationship between the two countries during the war years. Numbering 452 British women, 173 children and 1 bridegroom, they arrived in the United States on February 4, 1946. Like most war brides, they traveled to this country by ship. Before the expiration of the War Brides Act and other similar programs in December 1948, 300,000 women and dependents made their way to begin a new life in the United States.[275]

Many war brides were brought into the Wilds region. In March 1946, Mrs. Leonard Orcutt and Mrs. Joseph Zarnick, both from England and wives of GIs, arrived in Kane, McKean County. They traveled to the United States on the *Queen Mary*, docking in New York City. Mrs. Zarnick was formerly Jean Snow, and she and her husband were married in Leicester, England, in June 1944. She arrived with their infant daughter, Toni. Mrs. Orcutt, formerly Vida Carter, married her husband at Hanley, England, in December 1944. They reported an uneventful trip across the Atlantic with 2,235 other brides and babies, except for one rough day that resulted in sea sickness for Vida.[276]

In November 1946, two war brides, one from England and one from Brazil, were interviewed by a local newspaper. Ruth Martin Wisor was the only daughter of a rubber plantation owner, born in a small town on the border of Bolivia and Brazil. She completed her high school education in 1940. She entered a commercial school in secretarial courses but had a flair for art, which gave her an opportunity to enroll in Escola De Belas Artes. During this time, she offered her services to the USO as a volunteer staff member, a group composed almost completely of Americans. Her work took her by plane to many bases throughout the country, and it was on one of those trips that she met Roland Edward Wisor, who was on duty at a PX at a jungle base.

Agnes Morgan Wilson, another war bride, was from England. Born in 1925 near the town of Warrington, she met her future husband at a party at the home of a friend. Her future husband, Joseph Wilson, was in the U.S. Army Medical Corps, having served months of service in Germany and Africa.

At the time of the news articles, the two women were described as "petite bundles of femininity—one from the South American country of Brazil, and the other, a native of England—whose marriages to American GIs brought them to the United States and are now employed at the Plant of Sylvania Electric Products in Brookville."[277]

In Jersey Shore, Lycoming County, Anne Rose Larson, wife of William Larson, became the first county war bride to become a citizen of the United States, on May 6, 1947. A native of Great Britain, Anne met her husband in Durban, South Africa, when he was a member of the U.S. Army Air Corps. Her parents relocated to Africa, where she met William. Married in September 1942, she joined her husband in Jersey Shore in October 1943. The couple had two small children at the time of her citizenship.[278]

The GI Bill of Rights

The Servicemen's Readjustment Act of 1944, more commonly known as the GI Bill of Rights, was created to help veterans of World War II. The act came about in part because of the country's experience with returning World War I veterans striving to reenter civilian life. The numbers of returning servicemen was so great that their presence flooded the labor market, making many of them unemployed and struggling to make ends meet. As a stop-gap measure, Congress passed the Bonus Act of 1924, which promised veterans a bonus based on the number of days served. There was only one problem: the bonuses wouldn't be paid until 1945, twenty years later, too late to help the struggling veterans.[279]

The Great Depression brought the situation to a head. In the spring of 1932, between ten thousand and twenty-five thousand veterans, along with their wives and children, marched on the U.S. Capitol demanding their bonus money to alleviate the economic hardships being caused by the Great Depression. The marchers, sometimes called the "Bonus Expeditionary Force," moved into abandoned shacks below the Capitol and set up shanties and tents along the Anacostia River. In spite of their numbers and inadequate housing and food, order was maintained.[280]

In June, the U.S. House of Representatives passed a bill that authorized an immediate payout of the bonuses that the Senate promptly rejected. While a number of protestors returned home, it was estimated that somewhere between two thousand and ten thousand remained over the next few weeks to protest, causing restlessness and threats. In response to requests by local authorities, President Herbert Hoover called on Brigadier General Perry Miles, accompanied by General Douglas MacArthur, the U.S. Army chief of staff, to drive out the demonstrators and destroy their encampments. Using tanks and tear gas, one veteran was shot to death, with other veterans and policemen wounded. Congress appropriated $100,000 to send the protestors home.[281]

The actions of removing the Bonus Marchers was an unpopular move for Hoover, and those actions became a turning point in the crusade for veterans' rights. Franklin Roosevelt, who followed Hoover into office, wanted to do better for veterans returning from World War II, and he began to make preparations in advance of the end of the war. A former American Legion national commander and Republican national chairman, Harry W. Colmery, proposed extending benefits to all World War II veterans, male or female. The bill went to Congress in January 1944 and was hotly debated in both the House of Representatives and the Senate but was approved in mid-June. Roosevelt signed the GI Bill into law of June 22.[282]

The GI Bill included many benefits. Those who wished to continue their education in college or vocation school could do so tuition-free up to $500 while receiving a cost-of-living payment. The bill provided a weekly unemployment benefit for up to one year, and job counseling was made available. The government guaranteed loans for veterans who borrowed money to purchase a home, business or farm, and medical care was also provided. Hospitals were built for veterans, and the Veterans Administration took over all veteran-related concerns. In 1947, nearly 49 percent of college admissions were veterans.[283]

Speaking about the history of Penn State University and its experience with the GI Bill, Brian Clark, director of the Office of Veterans Programs at Penn State, noted in an interview in 2019, "Fear made us generous. We had to figure out a way to civilianize this population. If we didn't, we would have had anarchy. Institutions were adjusting to this, sort of, 'manna from heaven.' The effects of this were actually extraordinary. About a million people, mostly men, ended up getting college degrees who otherwise, most likely, never would have." Enrollment at Penn State in 1944 was 3,294, and by 1945, that number had jumped to 5,779, with enrollment standing at 10,563 in 1946. Enrollment continued to increase to a high of 14,970 in 1949.[284]

With the end of World War II and the adoption of the GI Bill of Rights that brought in massive numbers of veterans into University Park and the Penn State campus, trailers were brought in to the campus to serve as living quarters.

Brian Clark said of the increased enrollment, "Penn State went from being a little college to a major university. It wasn't just Penn State. All of the big universities got their jump-start following World War II and the influx of GI Bill recipients. So, it was a big deal."[285]

In 1945, the *Daily Gazette and Bulletin* in Williamsport, Pennsylvania, reported that the GI Bill of Rights had created an unheard-of situation in high schools, preparatory school and colleges. "Twenty-five years ago or even 10 years ago, a student over 25 years of age in college was an oddity on the campus. In high school, a boy or girl of 21 was somewhat of a freak. The GI Bill of Rights has altered this attitude. Through federal subsidies of $50 per month to single veterans and $75 per month to married veterans, also an innovation in American school and college life, men and women in their late twenties, thirties and forties are returning to college and overage veterans in their twenties are returning to high school to obtain diplomas."[286]

Top: "Windcrest, b&w, undated." *Photographic vertical files, Physical Plant (01184), used with permission from the Eberly Family Special Collections Library, Penn State University Libraries.*

Bottom: World War II GI students. "War, WWII/Misc. (b&w) 1941–1945." *Photographic vertical files, Events (01179), used with permission from the Eberly Family Special Collections Library, Penn State University Libraries.*

In 1945, the Williamsport Technical Institute had an enrollment of more than 130 veterans, enlisted men and officers, with drafting being the choice of study for most of the students, while others were enrolled in the machine shop, radio communications, electricity, auto mechanics and diesel engines and aviation mechanics.[287]

On January, 10, 1946, Clarion State Teachers College, later Clarion University, was advertising for living quarters for GI families. Two married veterans were looking for accommodations, and the college said there would be more requests when the second semester began on January 23. More than fifty single veterans were about to enter college during the second semester, and Egbert Hall, the men's dormitory that had been built in 1939, would be full for the first time since it was constructed. Another number would be rooming in the old dormitory on the third floor of the Science Hall, and the old dormitory on the third floor of Seminary Hall was already filled with married veterans' families. The college called on anyone in Clarion who was willing to rent small apartments or connecting rooms or even attic rooms to contact the college.[288]

While the GI Bill remains popular, it has evolved since it was first signed into law in 1944. Many in the Pennsylvania Wilds have benefited from this program.

The Baby Boomer Generation

There have been generational titles attached to groups of people in the United States for a number of years. People born between 1900 and 1924 are known as the "GI Generation," people born between 1925 to 1945 are known as the "Silent Generation," those born between 1946 and 1964 are identified as the "Boomer Generation" and those born between 1965 and 1980 are "Generation X," with various other group titles coming forward to today's present "Gen Alpha," those born between 2011 and 2024. Studies show that people lumped into these generational categories share similar characteristics and behaviors formed by their common experiences.

The Baby Boomer generation was marked by a dramatic increase in birth rates and prosperity following World War II. The Baby Boomer generation is part of one of the largest generations in U.S. history.[289]

In the 2010 federal census, 26.6 percent of Pennsylvania's population were of the Boomer Generation. Studies reveal that a large number of

Baby Boomers received high school diplomas and had attained a bachelor's degree or higher. Pennsylvania's Boomers were more likely to be married than Boomers in other areas of the United States.[290]

With the increase in population, school districts throughout the Wilds began construction of new buildings to accommodate the increased class sizes. Ridgway Area School District opened a new high school in the fall of 1961; seven new elementary schools opened in Warren County in 1961; a new Kane elementary school in McKean County opened in 1961; and a new high school opened in Coudersport, Potter County, and a new elementary school at Blossburg in Tioga County in 1953, just as the Boomers were entering their school age years.

The Boomers nationally had an influence on events in the country. Some were protestors during the Vietnam War, while others served their country. They were the Woodstock generation, the Summer of Love participants, the hippie generation. Through it all, the Greatest Generation wanted the best for their children.

Reflecting on Boomers from the past attending the Woodstock Music Festival, where it was estimated 400,000 people gathered on a six-hundred-acre farm for three days of music by their favorite artists such as Joan Baez, Janis Joplin, Jefferson Airplane, Sly and the Family Stone and Creedence Clearwater Revival, Charles Yank, the head of the police department in Monticello, New York, said, "Notwithstanding their personality, their dress and their ideas, they were and are the most courteous, considerate and well-behaved group of kids I have ever been in contact with during my 24 years of police work."[291]

But as with each generation, the Boomers grew up generally to become responsible citizens. In 2024, the youngest of the Boomer generation born in 1964 turned sixty years of age, while the earliest Boomers turned seventy-eight.

As one explores the Pennsylvania Wilds, many of the shop owners are of the Boomer generation. Politically, State Senators Chris Dush and Scott Hutchinson, who represent the Wilds region, are of the Boomer generation, as are State Representatives Kathy Rapp, Mike Armanini, Kerry Benninghoff and Jamie Flick. Glenn Thompson, representing the Fifteenth Congressional District in Washington for much of the Pennsylvania Wilds, is of the Boomer generation.

Home Construction

The numbers of Americans who served in the war are staggering. By the time the war ended in 1945, 50 million men had registered for the draft, and more than 10 million had served.[292]

With so many service members returning home, combined with a decrease in home building during the war years, an acute housing shortage was created in many areas. In some sections of the United States, Quonset huts were converted into homes. With a shortage of about 5 million homes in America, the government provided a stimulus to build new ones. In larger areas of the country, massive home building led to construction in the suburbs.[293]

It took years to catch up with home building. Many returning vets married, started families and lived with relatives until they could afford their own homes. Apartment living was common, and larger homes of twelve rooms or more were often converted into apartments to accommodate those needing housing.

In 1945, the *Jeffersonian-Democrat* in Brookville printed the following article about the shortage of homes in the coming year:

> *Shortage of Homes Is Hard on the Returning Vets*
> *The year 1946 will see an "acute and growing housing shortage" declares John B. Blandford, Jr., National Housing Administrator, who says that new construction will fill only a fraction of the urgent need.*
>
> *Excluding farm needs there are 1,200,000 families without housing facilities and an estimated 3,400,000 families, including 1,600,000 service men, will want homes by the end of the year.*
>
> *This is a serious situation, without much being done to remedy it. There is no lack of funds for construction, but, if there were, the various loans for home building could finance the construction needed. It is not comfortable to think that men who served overseas, now home after winning two great wars, should not be able to get the homes they desire.*[294]

The GI Bill provided returning veterans with low-interest mortgages, making homeownership more accessible, which allowed millions of veterans to purchase homes.

Within the Wilds, a boom in home construction didn't lead to the building of huge communities such as the one in Levittown in Bucks County, Pennsylvania, which between 1952 and 1958 built 17,311 homes, but there was a definite home building trend in the Wilds, with new sections being added to the long-established communities. As an example, in Ridgway, county seat of Elk County, a new section was opened up for home building, with construction of many homes in an area known as Dewey Circle just off Montmorenci Avenue.

In 1945, an enterprising builder advertised in the *Potter Enterprise* of Coudersport:

> *Veterans, Attention*
>
> *March Into Your Own Home*
>
> *Priorities and G.I. Loans*
> *Are Available for*
> *New Home Construction*
>
> *For Discharged Veterans*
> *of World War II*
>
> > *Plan a home to suit your personal taste—Built*
> > *new from the ground up by responsible local*
> > *building contractors, not pre-fabricated 1000 miles away.*
>
> *Complete One-Stop Service*
> *On*
> *Plans, Specifications, Lot sites,*
> *Reputable Building Contractors*
> *Financing and Government Regulations*
>
> *E.P. Huntington*
> *Coudersport, Phone 8*[295]

With the addition of new industry in Brookville, Jefferson County, a survey in 1956 revealed that more than thirty homes were in some stage of construction in the borough, with a dozen more within a few miles of town. The opening of subdivisions had encouraged home building.[296]

In Wellsboro, Tioga County, the Bastian Construction Company and West's Farm Agency announced the opening of the Ordway Development in the borough of Elkland, where seventeen building lots were offered with approved VA and FHA financing.[297]

There was a distinctive style to most of the homes being built during the postwar boom, and as one rides around the many communities located in the Wilds, those houses are easily identified. Generally of Cape Cod design or one-story ranch homes, a postwar home is most likely found in a large neighborhood and has a modest backyard. The homes often had less than one thousand square feet of living space, with a picture window at the front and a kitchen with a window and door facing the backyard. And unlike homes built before the war, most of the postwar homes had garages, as families more and more owned automobiles and relied on their own vehicles for transportation.[298]

Eventually, the veterans were accommodated and settled into raising their families. The Wilds returned to a state of "normalcy" with the end of rationing and industries returning to their prewar schedules of production.

CONCLUSION

As I was completing this book, the Wilds was honoring its service men and women on Veterans Day (previously called Armistice Day), November 11, 2024. It was a celebration marking the end of World War I in 1918. In 1954, the name Veterans Day came into use, appropriately honoring all of our veterans. At the Ridgway schools that I attended, we were called on to pause for a moment of silence on the eleventh hour of the eleventh day of the eleventh month, harkening back to the 1918 armistice, while also remembering all of our veterans from many conflicts.

As part of Veterans Day celebrations, a local newspaper interviewed Wilfred "Bud" Neubert, a 103-year-old veteran whom I met briefly on two occasions while participating in Wreaths Across America remembrance ceremonies in December at Beechwoods Cemetery outside of Falls Creek, Jefferson County.

Neubert was born in Elk County, Pennsylvania, in 1921 and enlisted in the navy when he was twenty-one years old. He served four years as a gunner's mate on five different merchant ships. Neubert's wartime experiences included travel to Africa and sailing up the Red Sea to Egypt. He recalled air raids, ships that were torpedoed and manning the guns on ship decks.[299]

When he returned from the war, he was employed at Stackpole Carbon Company in St. Marys before being joining Brockway Glass in Brockway, Pennsylvania, for forty years. He and his wife were the parents of two children, and he has two grandchildren and one great-grandchild.[300]

Neubert has been an active member of the Brockway community over the years. He was involved with hosting the Harvest of Love Dinners at Moorhead Methodist Church and was a volunteer for Meals on Wheels, delivering meals to local homebound people.[301]

Wilfred "Bud" Neubert, 103-year-old World War II vet, reflects on time in the service. *Brianne Fleming and the* Tri-County Weekend, *November 9–10, 2024.*

Reflecting on Neubert's life as reported in the news article, I believe he embodies the characteristics that defined the Greatest Generation, particularly commitment and self-sacrifice.

At 103 years old, he keeps busy. He is a member of the Brockway American Legion Post 95 and is the oldest member of the Brockway Volunteer Hose Company. Living at DuBois Village, he walks regularly on its grounds and on occasion visits residents at the DuBois Nursing Home. Neubert attends Veterans Day dinners at the Legion and enjoys attending the Veterans Day assembly at the Brockway school district, where veterans are recognized each year. He also participates in Wreathes Across America, including the most recent ceremony in December 2024.[302]

My parents and others in the Greatest Generation just got the job done. I can imagine there were complaints at times about gas rationing, food rationing and all of the controls that were put on the population, but what was the alternative? Had they not stepped up to fight on the battlefield and to sacrifice on the homefront, the United States could have easily been taken over by our enemies, and those of us who followed that generation might today be speaking German or Japanese, depending on which coast you live near. As it turned out, the Greatest Generation prevailed, and the United States became a dominant world power.

As I sorted through family photos from those years for use in this book, I realized that there was an emptiness in the photo album from about 1941 to 1946, when film for personal use may have been in short supply or the family simply could not afford to purchase film.

The Greatest Generation gave my generation a prosperous future. But the Wilds of World War II has changed. Many of the major industries of that day are gone, with new industries filling the void. Schools were expanded to accommodate the Baby Boomer generation. Colleges such as Penn State University and Lock Haven University branched out to open offsite Commonwealth campuses. Homeownership greatly expanded.

It must be incomprehensible to today's younger generations, who have almost instant access to news on their many devices, that their great-grandparents got their news over radios and watched war-related newsreels at the local theater. Or that their great-grandparents served in the military in the largest conflict in human history. Despite our complaints about restrictions during the recent COVID-19 pandemic, their great-grandparents sacrificed for years to make our country victorious.

To the Greatest Generation—we're proud to have known you!

NOTES

Preface

1. Pennsylvania Wilds, "About the Pennsylvania Wilds."
2. Pennsylvania Wilds, "About the Pennsylvania Wilds."

Part I

3. Britannica, "Greatest Generation."
4. Stanford, "Full Committee Hearing on Statement."
5. Britannica, "Greatest Generation."
6. Family Search, "Greatest Generation: Birth Years, Characteristics, and History."
7. Family Search, "Greatest Generation: Birth Years, Characteristics, and History."
8. National Archives, "Zimmermann Telegram."
9. National Archives, "Zimmermann Telegram."
10. History, "This Day in History: May 4, 1926."
11. *Brockway (PA) Record*, "United States May Break with Germany," 1.
12. National Archives, "Zimmermann Telegram."
13. *Brockway (PA) Record*, "Dastardly German Plot," 1.
14. Micek, "Century Ago."
15. Klein, "How Economic Turmoil After WWI."

16. State College News, "Gangsters to Grandmothers."
17. *Funk & Wagnalls New Encyclopedia*, "Prohibition in the United States," 382.
18. *Funk & Wagnalls New Encyclopedia*, "Prohibition in the United States," 383.
19. Britannica, "Prohibition."
20. Britannica, "Prohibition."
21. State College News, "Gangsters to Grandmothers."
22. State College News, "Gangsters to Grandmothers."
23. State College News, "Gangsters to Grandmothers."
24. Cox, "Shore Lines," 3.
25. Cox, "Shore Lines," 3.
26. Cox, "Shore Lines," 3.
27. Britannica, "Prohibition."
28. Britannica, "Prohibition."
29. *Potter Enterprise*, "End Comes Quickly," 6.
30. Ayers, "As I Knew Eliot Ness," 40.
31. *Potter Enterprise*, "Walter Taylor Reminisces," 1.
32. *Potter Enterprise*, "Walter Taylor Reminisces," 1.
33. *Warren (PA) Times Mirror*, "Flapper Evolves," 4.
34. *Brookville (PA) Republican*, "Electricity for the Farm," 3.
35. History, "Roaring Twenties."
36. *Punxsutawney (PA) News*, "Decade Brings Vast Radio Change," 5.
37. History, "Roaring Twenties."
38. *Clarion (PA) Democrat*, "Chevrolet Is Superior," 7.
39. *Clarion (PA) Democrat*, "Garage Is an Interesting Place!," 6.
40. *Punxsutawney (PA) Spirit*, "No Business Depression Is Feared," 7.
41. History, "What Caused the Great Depression?"
42. History, "What Caused the Great Depression?"
43. History, "What Caused the Great Depression?"
44. History, "What Caused the Great Depression?"
45. *Warren (PA) Times Mirror*, "Cooperation Needed," 1.
46. *Warren (PA) Times Mirror*, "Cooperation Needed," 1.
47. History, "What Caused the Great Depression?"
48. Living New Deal Projects by State and City.
49. Living New Deal Projects by State and City.
50. Living New Deal Projects by State and City.
51. Living New Deal Projects by State and City.
52. History, "What Caused the Great Depression?"
53. History, "Civilian Conservation Corps."
54. Byers, "CCC Boys of the Pennsylvania Wilds."

55. Department of Conservation and Natural Resources, "Civilian Conservation Corps."
56. Byers, "CCC Boys of the Pennsylvania Wilds."
57. Byers, "CCC Boys of the Pennsylvania Wilds."
58. Byers, "CCC Boys of the Pennsylvania Wilds."
59. Byers, "CCC Boys of the Pennsylvania Wilds."
60. Byers, "CCC Boys of the Pennsylvania Wilds."
61. Byers, "CCC Boys of the Pennsylvania Wilds."
62. *Brockway (PA) Record*, "God Bless America," 3.
63. *Punxsutawney (PA) Spirit*, "House Prepares to Pass Vinson Navy Bill," 1.
64. Global Security, "Ship Building 1933–45—Roosevelt, Franklin, D."
65. Global Security, "Ship Building 1933–45—Roosevelt, Franklin, D."
66. Global Security, "Ship Building 1933–45—Roosevelt, Franklin, D."
67. Global Security, "Ship Building 1933–45—Roosevelt, Franklin, D."
68. *Funk & Wagnalls New Encyclopedia*, "Lend-Lease," 141–42.
69. *Funk & Wagnalls New Encyclopedia*, "Lend-Lease," 141–42.

Part II

70. National Air and Space Museum/Smithsonian, "Complicated Lead Up to Pearl Harbor."
71. *Funk & Wagnalls New Encyclopedia*, "Pearl Harbor," 369.
72. *Funk & Wagnalls New Encyclopedia*, "Pearl Harbor," 370.
73. *Warren (PA) Times Mirror*, "Remember Pearl Harbor," 4.
74. *Express*, "Centre, Lycoming Boys Killed in Hawaii Attack," 5.
75. *Warren (PA) Times Mirror*, "Former Barnes Youth Hurt in Hawaii Action," 9.
76. *Punxsutawney (PA) Spirit*, "Brookville Man Comes Thru," 2.
77. *Punxsutawney (PA) Spirit*, "Washington," 1.
78. Explore PA History, "Stories from Pennsylvania History."
79. Explore PA History, "Stories from Pennsylvania History."

Part III

80. *Express*, "Big Recruiting Boom Here and All Over the Nation."
81. *Brockway (PA) Record*, "Married Men May Enlist," 11.
82. *Jeffersonian-Democrat*, "Navy Enlistments at DuBois Increase," 6.

83. *Warren (PA) Times Mirror*, "Conscientious Objectors."
84. *Warren (PA) Times Mirror*, "Conscientious Objectors."
85. *Wellsboro Gazette Combined with Mansfield Advertiser*, "Explanation," 3.
86. *Punxsutawney (PA) Spirit*, "Draft Boards Notified," 1.
87. North-Central Pennsylvania, "Clinton County Woman's WWII Service Honored."
88. North-Central Pennsylvania, "Clinton County Woman's WWII Service Honored."
89. *Sykesville (PA) Post-Dispatch*, "Nurses Are Needed for Service," 10.
90. NavSource Online, "Army Ship Photo Archive, USAHS Marigold."
91. *Ridgway (PA) Record*, "Anne Marie Hargrave."
92. History, "This Day in History: FDR Proclaims an Unlimited National Emergency."
93. History, "This Day in History: FDR Proclaims an Unlimited National Emergency."
94. Stevens, "Pennsylvania's First Year in World War II," 97–98.
95. Pennsylvania Historic Preservation, "Preservation Backstory."
96. Pennsylvania Historic Preservation, "Preservation Backstory."
97. Pennsylvania Historic Preservation, "Preservation Backstory."
98. *Kane (PA) Republican*, "Girl's Town," 4.
99. *Kane (PA) Republican*, "Girl's Town," 4.
100. *Kane (PA) Republican*, "Girl's Town," 4.
101. Wessman, "History of Elk County, Pennsylvania, 1981," 177–78.
102. *Kane (PA) Republican*, "Girl's Town," 4.
103. *Kane (PA) Republican*, "Girl's Town," 4.
104. *Kane (PA) Republican*, "Girl's Town," 4.
105. *Kane (PA) Republican*, "Girl's Town," 4.
106. *Kane (PA) Republican*, "Girl's Town," 4.
107. *Kane (PA) Republican*, "One Killed in Explosion at Eldred Plant," 1.
108. Cheney, "Uncovering PA."
109. Close, "Duke Center Native Zetler."
110. Close, "Duke Center Native Zetler."
111. Close, "Duke Center Native Zetler."
112. Close, "Duke Center Native Zetler."
113. Close, "Duke Center Native Zetler."
114. *Lancaster (PA) New Era*, "Ernie Pyle," 8.
115. Zippo, "Our History."
116. Zippo, "Our History."

117. *Bradford Evening Star and the Bradford Daily Record*, "900 Zippo Lighters Sent to Men," 6.
118. *Lewisburg (PA) Journal*, "Early Settlers," 3.
119. *Patriot News*, "State Hosted Top-Secret WWII Site," 6.
120. *Shamokin (PA) News-Dispatch*, "Shamokin Group Tours U.S. Plant," 5.
121. *Shamokin (PA) News-Dispatch*, "Shamokin Group Tours U.S. Plant," 5.
122. *Sunbury (PA) Daily Item*, "Counselor to Assist Valley Plant Women," 2.
123. *Shamokin (PA) News-Dispatch*, "Shamokin Group Tours U.S. Plant," 5.
124. *Shamokin (PA) News-Dispatch*, "Shamokin Group Tours U.S. Plant," 5.
125. *Sunbury (PA) Daily Item*, "POW Guards Win Army 'E,'" 4.
126. *Canton (PA) Independent-Sentinel*, "Pennsylvania Ordnance Works Is Closed," 1.
127. *Patriot News*, "State Hosted Top-Secret WWII Site," 6.
128. *Patriot News*, "State Hosted Top-Secret WWII Site," 6.
129. *Patriot News*, "State Hosted Top-Secret WWII Site," 6.
130. *Patriot News*, "State Hosted Top-Secret WWII Site," 6.
131. Muncy Historical Society, "Call to Action."
132. Piper Aircraft, "Brief History of Piper Aircraft."
133. Novell, "World War II and the Piper Cub."
134. Novell, "World War II and the Piper Cub."
135. Novell, "World War II and the Piper Cub."
136. *Express*, "Germans Fear Cubs," 5.
137. *Arizona Republic*, "Conflict Opens New Frontiers," 22.
138. *Express*, "W.T. Piper Speaks at WASP Exercises," 1.
139. *Express*, "W.T. Piper Speaks at WASP Exercises," 1.
140. WNEP, "World War II Pilot Shares Stories."
141. Reiff, "Pieces of the Past."
142. *Warren (PA) Times Mirror*, "Boost for Local Plant," 4.
143. *Warren (PA) Times Mirror*, "Boost for Local Plant," 4.
144. *Times Observer*, "End of the Line."
145. *Warren (PA) Times Mirror*, "Enthusiasm of Workers Commended," 1.

Part IV

146. *Brockway (PA) Record*, "Flash from China," 1.
147. *Brockway (PA) Record*, "Going to China," 1.
148. *Brockway (PA) Record*, "Monday Chapel Program," 3.

149. History, "This Day in History: February 15, 1942."
150. *Brockway (PA) Record*, "Monday Chapel Program."
151. *Brockway (PA) Record*, "Dear Ralph," July 16, 1943, 8.
152. *Brockway (PA) Record*, "Dear Ralph," November 12, 1943, 8.
153. *Brockway (PA) Record*, "Dear Ralph," January 28, 1944, 8.
154. *Brockway (PA) Record*, "Dear Ralph," March 3, 1944, 8.
155. U.S. National Park Service, "World War II Home Front."
156. *Punxsutawney (PA) Spirit*, "Formation of a Civil Defense Force," 1.
157. *Centre Daily Times*, "101 Register for Civil Defense in Bfte. Area," 1.
158. *Mansfield (PA) Advertiser*, "Call for Volunteers as Air Raid Wardens," 1.
159. *Wellsboro Gazette Combined with Mansfield Advertiser*, "Blackout All Night Tonight," 1.
160. *Wellsboro Gazette Combined with Mansfield Advertiser*, "Blackout All Night Tonight," 1.
161. U.S. National Park Service, "World War II Home Front."
162. U.S. National Park Service, "World War II Home Front."
163. *Kane (PA) Republican*, "President Asks Everyone to Grow Victory Garden," 3.
164. *Kane (PA) Republican*, "President Asks Everyone to Grow Victory Garden," 3.
165. *Punxsutawney (PA) Spirit*, "WPA Victory Gardens Produce Tons," 1.
166. *Punxsutawney (PA) Spirit*, "WPA Victory Gardens Produce Tons," 1.
167. *Warren (PA) Times Mirror*, "Home Canners Urged to Fill Jars," 10.
168. National World War II Museum, "Rationing."
169. *Warren (PA) Times Mirror*, "Chairmen Are Named by Tire Ration Boards," 12.
170. *Warren (PA) Times Mirror*, "Chairmen Are Named by Tire Ration Boards," 12.
171. *Wellsboro (PA) Agitator*, "Tire Rationing in Effect Soon," 8.
172. *Wellsboro (PA) Agitator*, "Tire Rationing in Effect Soon," 8.
173. *Courier-Express* "Today in History."
174. *Jeffersonian-Democrat*, "County Cattle Said to Be Aiding Black Market," 1.
175. National World War II Museum, "Take a Closer Look at War Bonds."
176. National World War II Museum, "Take a Closer Look at War Bonds."
177. National World War II Museum, "Take a Closer Look at War Bonds."
178. *Mansfield (PA) Advertiser*, "Deliver Us from Evil, Buy War Bonds," 3.
179. *Funk & Wagnalls New Encyclopedia*, "Poliomyelitis," 228, 230.
180. *Funk & Wagnalls New Encyclopedia*, "Poliomyelitis," 228, 230.
181. Historical Society of Pennsylvania, "Polio in Pennsylvania."

182. *Kane (PA) Republican*, "Potter, Tioga Area in Polio Outbreak," 1.
183. *Patriot News*, "State Polio Cases Now Number 1338," 4.
184. *Kane (PA) Republican*, "All of Ludlow Under Two Week Quarantine," 1.
185. *Punxsutawney (PA) Spirit*, "DuBois Uses Curfew as Check to Polio," 7.
186. Britannica, "Elizabeth Kenny, Australian Nurse."
187. Britannica, "Elizabeth Kenny, Australian Nurse."
188. *Kane (PA) Republican*, "Four McKean Nurses," 6.
189. *Kane (PA) Republican*, "Kane Surrounded by Nazis," 28.
190. *Warren (PA) Times Mirror*, "Army Takes Over Camp," 7.
191. *Warren (PA) Times Mirror*, "Army Takes Over Camp," 7.
192. *Warren (PA) Times Mirror*, "Contingent of Prisoners Reaches Kane," 5.
193. *Warren (PA) Times Mirror*, "Contingent of Prisoners Reaches Kane," 5.
194. *Kane (PA) Republican*, "Kane Surrounded by Nazis."
195. *Potter Enterprise*, "German War Prisoners Cut Wood," 4.
196. *Kane (PA) Republican*, "Open Secret," 4.
197. *Kane (PA) Republican*, "Open Secret," 4.
198. *Warren (PA) Times Mirror*, "War Prisoners Rounded Up," 2.
199. *Kane (PA) Republican*, "Two Nazi POWs on the Loose," 3.
200. *Kane (PA) Republican*, "German Prisoner of War Returns," 4.
201. *Kane (PA) Republican*, "After 32 Years," 3.
202. *Kane (PA) Republican*, "After 32 Years," 3.
203. *Kane (PA) Republican*, "Return to Camp Marienville," 10.
204. *Kane (PA) Republican*, "Return to Camp Marienville," 10.

Part V

205. *Tri-County Weekend*, "World War II Vet Remembers D-Day," 13.
206. Holwitt, "Recapturing the Interwar Navy's Strategic Magic."
207. Ancestry, "Wilbur Joseph Jackson."
208. Navy History, "Naval History and Heritage Command, *Canopus*."
209. Navy History, "Naval History and Heritage Command, *Canopus*."
210. Allied POWs in Japan, "American Prisoners of War in the Philippines."
211. Allied POWs in Japan, "American Prisoners of War in the Philippines."
212. Allied POWs in Japan, "Bilibid POW Camp, Manila, Philippines."
213. Allied POWs in Japan, "American Prisoners of War in the Philippines."

214. *Kane (PA) Republican*, "In a Paragraph," May 14, 1943, 2.
215. *Kane (PA) Republican*, "In a Paragraph," April 20, 1945, 2.
216. *Sacramento (CA) Bee*, "Obituary for Wilbur Joseph Jackson."
217. North, letter sent to Myers family.
218. *Courier-Express*, "Hometown Heroes, Military Salute."
219. Pacific Wrecks, "Owi Airfield, Biak Numfor Regency."
220. Army Air Corps Library and Museum, "22nd Bombardment Group."
221. Ancestry, "Missing Aircrew Report."
222. Pierce, "Sandakan Paints a Portrait of Hell on Earth."
223. Gin, "Japanese Occupation of Borneo."
224. *Courier-Express*, "Hometown Heroes, Military Salute."
225. Beague, "PA Airman Killed in World War II."
226. Beague, "PA Airman Killed in World War II."
227. *Williamsport (PA) Sun-Gazette*, "Lieut. Litherland Missing Over France," 3.
228. U.S. National Park Service, "U.S. Air Force Strategic Air Command."
229. Ancestry, James Litherland military records.
230. Cambridge Military History, "RAF, Molesworth."
231. 303rd Bomb Group, "Hells Angels."
232. *Williamsport (PA) Sun-Gazette*, "South Williamsport WWII Casualty Identified."
233. *Williamsport (PA) Sun-Gazette*, "South Williamsport WWII Casualty Identified."
234. *Williamsport (PA) Sun-Gazette*, "South Williamsport WWII Casualty Identified."
235. Beague, "PA Airman Killed in World War II."
236. Beague, "PA Airman Killed in World War II."
237. *Bradford Evening Star and the Bradford Daily Record*, "William J. Price Radio Message," 9.
238. *Bradford Evening Star and the Bradford Daily Record*, "Heinie Price May Be Captive of Jap Forces," 1.
239. *Bradford Evening Star and the Bradford Daily Record*, "Heinie Price May Be Captive of Jap Forces," 1.
240. *Bradford Evening Star and the Bradford Daily Record*, "W.J. Price Transferred from Philippines," 3.
241. Allied POWs in Japan, "History of the Osaka Main Camp—Chikko."
242. Kovner, "Prisoners of the Empire."
243. *Bradford (PA) Era*, "W.J. Price, 27, Home After 4 Years Prison," 1.
244. Find a Grave, "William J. Price and Mary Jane Grandin Price."

245. Mount Zion Historical Society, "Remembering: Clark Ralph Ingram."
246. Mount Zion Historical Society, "Remembering: Clark Ralph Ingram."
247. Ancestry, Clark Ralph Ingram Draft Card.
248. Mount Zion Historical Society, "Remembering: Clark Ralph Ingram."
249. *Daily News*, "PA Soldiers Missing in Six Fighting Areas," 2.
250. O'Donnell, *Shoe Leather Express*, preface.
251. O'Donnell, *Shoe Leather Express*, preface.
252. *Daily Gazette and Bulletin*, "Francis Kennedy Wounded in Italy," 19.
253. NPR, "World War II Stories on NPR: Battle on the Slopes."
254. NPR, "World War II Stories on NPR: Battle on the Slopes."
255. *Williamsport (PA) Sun-Gazette*, "Francis Kennedy."
256. *Williamsport (PA) Sun-Gazette*, "Francis Kennedy."
257. NPR, "World War II Stories on NPR: Battle on the Slopes."
258. *Williamsport (PA) Sun-Gazette*, "Francis Kennedy."
259. Find a Grave, "Francis Xavier Kennedy."
260. *Williamsport (PA) Sun-Gazette*, "Francis Kennedy."
261. Find a Grave, "Francis Xavier Kennedy."

Part VI

262. *Funk & Wagnalls New Encyclopedia*, "World War II," 294–96.
263. *Funk & Wagnalls New Encyclopedia*, "World War II," 294–96.
264. *Warren (PA) Times Mirror*, "Former Times-Mirror Staff Member," 5.
265. *Mansfield (PA) Advertiser*, "Pvt Gordon Rose Writes of V-E Day Observance," 1.
266. History, "V-J Day History."
267. History, "V-J Day History."
268. History, "V-J Day History."

Part VII

269. Seiler, Marcus and Benjamin, "When the Lights Go On Again."
270. *Warren (PA) Times Mirror*, "Chandlers Valley," 5.
271. *Sykesville (PA) Post-Dispatch*, "World War II Ended Tuesday," 1.
272. *Jeffersonian-Democrat*, "Paul D. Shaffer Writes of Itinerary," 7.
273. *Potter Enterprise*, "Letters from Niver Brothers," 8.
274. National World War II Museum, "Coming to America."

275. National World War II Museum, "Coming to America."
276. *Kane (PA) Republican*, "British Brides of Kane Men," 1.
277. *Jefferson-Democrat*, "War Brides, from England and Brazil."
278. *Williamsport (PA) Sun-Gazette*, "War Bride Among Group," 5.
279. History, "GI Bill."
280. Britannica, "Bonus Army."
281. Britannica, "Bonus Army."
282. History, "GI Bill."
283. History, "GI Bill."
284. Penn State University, "For Many Veterans."
285. Penn State University, "For Many Veterans."
286. *Daily Gazette and Bulletin*, "Education News," 5.
287. *Daily Gazette and Bulletin*, "Education News," 5.
288. *Clarion (PA) Democrat*, "College Seeking Living Quarters for GI Families," 1.
289. Research Brief, "Pennsylvania's Oldest Baby Boomers Turn 65."
290. Research Brief, "Pennsylvania's Oldest Baby Boomers Turn 65."
291. *Warren (PA) Times Mirror*, "Last of Hippie Horde Departs from Festival," 2.
292. U.S. National Park Service, "American Home Front After World War II."
293. U.S. National Park Service, "American Home Front After World War II."
294. *Jeffersonian-Democrat*, "Shortage of Homes," 13.
295. *Potter Enterprise*, "Veterans, Attention," 4.
296. *Jeffersonian-Democrat*, "Brookville Is in Midst," 18.
297. *Wellsboro (PA) Agitator*, "New Ordway Housing Development," 1.
298. HGTV, "All About Post-War Architecture."

Conclusion

299. Fleming, "WWII Veteran at DuBois Village," 1.
300. Fleming, "WWII Veteran at DuBois Village," 1.
301. Fleming, "WWII Veteran at DuBois Village," 1.
302. Fleming, "WWII Veteran at DuBois Village," 1.

BIBLIOGRAPHY

Allied POWs in Japan. "American Prisoners of War in the Philippines—Office of the Provost Marshal General Report, November 19, 1945." http://www.mansell.com/pow_resources/camplists/philippines/pows_in_pi-OPMG_report.html.

———. "Bilibid POW Camp, Manila, Philippines."

———. "History of the Osaka Main Camp—Chikko."

Ancestry. Clark Ralph Ingram Draft Card. www.ancestry.com.

———. James Litherland military records. www.ancestry.com.

———. "Missing Aircrew Report," declassified, John T. North. www.ancestry.com.

———. "Wilbur Joseph Jackson, in the U.S., World War II Prisoners of the Japanese, 1941–1945." www.ancestry.com.

Arizona Republic. "Conflict Opens New Frontiers in Diverse Fields for Women." January 4, 1942.

Army Air Corps Library and Museum. "22nd Bombardment Group." https://www.armyaircorpsmuseum.org/22nd_Bombardment_Group.cfm.

Ayers, William J. "As I Knew Eliot Ness." *Potter Enterprise* (Coudersport, PA), November 24, 1971.

Beague, John. "PA Airman Killed in World War II Welcomed Home, Buried with Military Honors." PennLive, September 9, 2023. https://www.pennlive.com/news/2023/09/pa-airman-killed-in-world-war-ii-welcomed-home-buried-with-military-honors.html.

Bradford Evening Star and the Bradford Daily Record. "Heinie Price May Be Captive of Jap Forces." May 12, 1942.

———. "900 Zippo Lighters Sent to Men on Ernie Pyle's Ship." May 17, 1945.

———. "W.J. Price Transferred from Philippines to Prison Camp in Japan." January 5, 1945.

———. "William J. Price Radio Message Is Heard from Japan." March 28, 1945.

Bradford (PA) Era. "W.J. Price, 27, Home After 4 Years Prison." October 10, 1945.

Britannica. "Bonus Amy." https://www.britannica.com/event/Bonus-Army.

———. "Elizabeth Kenny, Australian Nurse." https:www.britannica.com/biography/Elizabeth-Kenny.

———. "The Greatest Generation." https://www.britannica.com/topic/Greatest-Generation.

———. "Prohibition." https://www.britannica.com/event/Prohibition-United-States-history-1920-1933.

Brockway (PA) Record. "Dastardly German Plot." March 2, 1917.

———. "Dear Ralph." July 16, 1943; November 12, 1943; January 28, 1944; March 3, 1944.

———. "Flash from China." December 19, 1941.

———. "God Bless America Is Song of Peace, Thanks." November 22, 1940.

———. "Going to China." February 22, 1935.

———. "Married Men May Enlist." December 19, 1941.

———. "Monday Chapel Program." January 1, 1943.

———. "United States May Break with Germany." February 2, 1917.

Brookville (PA) Republican. "Electricity for the Farm." September 6, 1923.

Byers, Ed. "The CCC Boys of the Pennsylvania Wilds: A Legacy Lives On." Pennsylvania Wilds, July 26, 2019. https://pawilds.com/ccc-boys-pennsylvania-wilds.

Cambridge Military History. "RAF, Molesworth. https://cambridgemilitaryhistory.com/2014/12/23/raf-molesworth-and-the-303rd-bombardment-group-heavy.

Canton (PA) Independent-Sentinel. "Pennsylvania Ordnance Works Is Closed." January 20, 1944.

Centre Daily Times (State College, PA). "101 Register for Civil Defense in Bfte. Area." December 19, 1941.

Cheney, Jim. "The Surprisingly Amazing Eldred World War II Museum." Uncovering PA. https://uncoveringpa.com/eldred-world-war-two-museum.

Clarion (PA) Democrat. "Chevrolet Is Superior." October 5, 1922.

———. "College Seeking Living Quarters for GI Families." January 10, 1946.

———. "A Garage Is an Interesting Place!" November 13, 1930.

Close, Barb. *Bradford (PA) Era*. "Duke Center Native Zetler Recalls Working at National Munitions Plant in Eldred." https://www.bradfordera.com/news/duke-center-native-zetler-recalls-working-at-national-munitions-plant-in-eldred/article_d6ead42c-6880-11e4-a5fb-0743fe86f1d9.html.

Courier-Express (DuBois, PA). "Hometown Heroes, Military Salute 2016, the North Family." November 2016.

———. "Today in History." February 7, 2023.

Cox, Joseph. "Shore Lines." *The Express* (Lock Haven, PA), September 25, 1968.

Daily Gazette and Bulletin (Williamsport, PA). "Education News." November 13, 1945.

———. "Francis Kennedy Wounded in Italy." March 9, 1945.

Daily News (Lebanon, PA). "PA Soldiers Missing in Six Fighting Areas." October 9, 1943.

Department of Conservation and Natural Resources. "The Civilian Conservation Corps." https://www.pa.gov/agencies/dcnr/recreation/where-to-go/state-parks/history/ccc-years.html.

Explore PA History. "Stories from Pennsylvania History." https://explorepahistory.com/stories.php.

The Express (Lock Haven, PA). "Big Recruiting Boom Here and All Over the Nation." December 12, 1941.

———. "Centre, Lycoming Boys Killed in Hawaii Attack." December 11, 1941.

———. "Germans Fear Cubs, Knowing They Mean Artillery Fire." March 1, 1944.

———. "W.T. Piper Speaks at WASP Exercises." October 30, 1943.

Family Search. "The Greatest Generation: Birth Years, Characteristics, and History." www.family-search.org/en/blog/greatest.

Find a Grave. "Francis Xavier Kennedy." https://www.findagrave.com.

———. "William J. Price and Mary Jane Grandin Price." https://www.findagrave.com.

Fleming, Brianna. "WWII Veteran at DuBois Village Reflects on Time in the Service at 103 Years Old." *Tri-County Weekend* (DuBois, PA), November 9-10, 2024.

Funk & Wagnalls New Encyclopedia. "Lend-Lease." Vol. 15. Funk & Wagnalls Inc., 1975.

———. "Poliomyelitis." Vol. 19. Funk & Wagnalls Inc., 1975.

———. "Prohibition in the United States." Funk & Wagnalls Inc., 1975.

———. Vol. 19. Funk & Wagnalls Inc., 1975.

———. "World War II." Vol. 25. Funk & Wagnalls Inc., 1975.

Gin, Ooi Keat. "The Japanese Occupation of Borneo." Rutledge/Taylor & Francis Group, London (2010), 96, 97.

Global Security. "Ship Building 1933–45—Roosevelt, Franklin, D." https://www.globalsecurity.org/military/systems/ship/scn-1933-roosevelt.htm.

HGTV. "All About Post-War Architecture." https://www.hgtv.com/design/decorating/design-101/all-about-post-war-architecture.

Historical Society of Pennsylvania. "Polio in Pennsylvania." https://hsp.org/blogs/fondly-pennsylvania/polio-pennsylvania.

History. "Civilian Conservation Corps." https://www.history.com/topics/great-depression/civilian-conservation-corps.

———. "GI Bill." https://www.history.com/topics/world-war-ii/gi-bill.

———. "The Roaring Twenties." https://www.history.com/topics/roaring-twenties-history.

———. "This Day in History: FDR Proclaims an Unlimited National Emergency in Response to Nazi Threats." https://www.history.com/this-day-in-history/fdr-proclaims-an-unlimited-national-emergency.

———. "This Day in History: February 15, 1942, Singapore Falls to Japan." https://www.history.com/this-day-in-history/singapore-falls-to-japan.

———. "This Day in History: May 4, 1926, Germany Agrees to Limit Its Submarine Warfare." https://www.history.com/this-day-in-history/germany-agrees-to-limit-its-submarine-warfare.

———. "V-J Day History." https://www.history.com/topics/world-war-ii/v-j-day.

———. "What Caused the Great Depression?" htts://www.history.com/topics/great-depression/great-depression-history.

Holwitt, Joel, Lieutenant Commander, U.S. Navy. "Recapturing the Interwar Navy's Strategic Magic." *Naval History Magazine* 31, no. 5 (October 2017). https://www.usni.org/magazines/naval-history-magazine/2017/october/recapturing-interwar-navys-strategic-magic.

Indiana University of Pennsylvania. "Indiana State Teachers College, 1930, Oak Yearbook, Elsa Youngdahl."

Jeffersonian-Democrat (Brookville, PA). "Brookville Is In Midst of Building Boom, Industrial, and in New Homes Constructed." December 13, 1956.

———. "County Cattle Said to Be Aiding Black Market." April 22, 1943.

———. "Navy Enlistments at DuBois Increase." January 22, 1942.

———. "Paul D. Shaffer Writes of Itinerary through Pacific." October 4, 1945.

———. "Shortage of Homes Is Hard on the Returning Vets." December 6, 1945.

———. "War Brides, from England and Brazil, Work Here." November 28, 1946.

Kane (PA) Republican. "Admiral Presents Army-Navy Award to Elliott Company." March 30, 1943.

———. "After 32 Years, German POW Returns." September 5, 1978.

———. "All of Ludlow Under Two Week Quarantine." August 5, 1944.

———. "British Brides of Kane Men in US, One Has Daughter." March 4, 1945.

———. "Four McKean Nurses Go to Tioga County to Fight Polio." August 8, 1944.

———. "German Prisoner of War Returns." August 13, 1955.

———. "Girl's Town." November 18, 1942.

———. "In a Paragraph." May 14, 1943; April 20, 1945.

———. "Kane Surrounded by Nazis." August 31, 1946.

———. "One Killed in Explosion at Eldred Plant." March 26, 1943.

———. "An Open Secret." January 29, 1945.

———. "Potter, Tioga Area in Polio Outbreak." August 8, 1944.

———. "President Asks Everyone to Grow Victory Garden." April 14, 1944.

———. "Return to Camp Marienville." September 11, 1993.

———. "Two Nazi POWs on the Loose." December 31, 1945.

Klein, Christopher. "How Economic Turmoil After WWI Led to the Great Depression." History, March 28, 2023, https://www.history.com/news/world-war-1-cause-great-depression.

Kovner, Sarah. "Prisoners of the Empire: Inside Japanese POW Camps." Harvard University, Oxford Academic. https://academic.oup..com/ssjj/article-abstract/26/1/125/6839387?redirectedFrom=fulltext.

Lancaster (PA) New Era. "Ernie Pyle: Our Top Commanders Labor Endlessly," May 30, 1944, 8.

Lewisburg (PA) Journal. "The Early Settlers." July 24, 1914, 3.

Living New Deal Projects by State and City. https://livingnewdeal.org/maps-and-sites/sites-by-state-and-city.

Mansfield (PA) Advertiser. "Call for Volunteers as Air Raid Wardens." December 10, 1941, 1.

———. "Deliver Us from Evil, Buy War Bonds." July 7, 1943, 3.

———. "Pvt. Gordon Rose Writes of V-E Day Observance." June 6, 1945.

Micek, John L. "A Century Ago, Pennsylvania Played a Key Role in World War I." PennLive, April 16, 2017. https://www.pennlive.com/opinion/2017/04/a_century_ago_pennsylvania_pla.html.

Mount Zion Historical Society. "Remembering: Clark Ralph Ingram." https://veterans.mtzionhistoricalsociety.org/veterans-list/clark-ralph-ingram.

Muncy Historical Society. "A Call to Action: Say 'No' to Alvira Land Swap." https://www.muncyhistoricalsociety.org/a-call-to-action-say-no-to-alvira-land-swap.

National Air and Space Museum/Smithsonian. "The Complicated Lead Up to Pearl Harbor." https://airandspace.si.edu/stories/editorial/complicated-lead-pearl-harbor.

National Archives. "The Zimmermann Telegram." https://www.archives.gov/milestone-documents/zimmermann-telegram.

National World War II Museum. "Coming to America: The War Brides Act of 1945." https://www.naionalww2museum.org/war/articles/war-brides-act-1945.

———. "Rationing." https://www.nationalww2museum.org/war/articles/rationing-during-wwii.

———. "Take a Close Look at War Bonds." http://enroll.nationalww2museum.org/learn/education/for-students/ww2-history/take-a-closer-look/war -bonds.html.

NavSource Online. "Army Ship Photo Archive, USAHS *Marigold*." https://www.navsource.org/archives/armyidx.htm.

Navy History. "Naval History and Heritage Command, *Canopus* (AS-9), 1922–1942." https://www.history.navy.mil/research/histories/ship-histories/danfs/c/canopus.html.

North-Central Pennsylvania. "Clinton County Woman's WWII Service Honored for Women's Army Corps Anniversary." https://www.northcentralpa.com/news/local/clinton-county-womans-wwii-service-honored-for-womens-army-corps-anniversary/article_2ad995f4-0e7c-11ef-8dce-9bd662ef6127.html.

North, John T., 33570077, Flight A, 355th Tech. Scho. Squadron. Letter sent to Myers family from Jefferson Barracks, Missouri, February 14, 1943. In possession of his cousin John Myers.

Novell, Robert. "World War II and the Piper Cub." https://www.robertnovell.com/blogworld-war-ii-and-piper-cub-april-23-2014.

NPR. "World War II Stories on NPR: Battle on the Slopes: World War II's Ski Troops." https://www.npr.org/2007/09/21/14594652/battle-on-the-slopes-world-war-iis-ski-troops.

O'Donnell, Joseph P. *The Shoe Leather Express, February 6, 1945, to May 2, 1945, 86 Days*. Triangle Reprocenter of Hamilton, 1982.

Pacific Wrecks. "Owi Airfield, Biak Numfor Regency." https://pacificwrecks.com/airfields/indonesia/owi/index-html.

Patriot News (Harrisburg, PA). "State Hosted Top-Secret WWII Site." March 3, 2015.

———. "State Polio Cases Now Number 1338." October 25, 1944.

Penn State University. "For Many Veterans, the GI Bill Is 'Life-Changing.'" https://www.psu.edu/impact/story/many-veterans-gi-bill-life-changing.

Pennsylvania Historic Preservation. "Preservation Backstory: Emporium's Sylvania Corporation Marker." https://pahistoricpreservation.com/preservation-backstory-emporiums-sylvania-corporation-marker.

Pennsylvania Wilds. "About the Pennsylvania Wilds." https://pawilds.com/about.

Pierce, Pete. "Sandakan Paints a Portrait of Hell on Earth." *The Australian*, November 10, 2012. https://www.theaustralian.com.au/arts/review/sandakan-paints-a-portrait-of-hell-on-earth/story-fn9n8gph-1226513615645#.

Piper Aircraft. "A Brief History of Piper Aircraft." https://www.piper.com/blog/piper-history.

Potter Enterprise (Coudersport, PA). "End Comes Quickly." May 23.1957.

———. "German War Prisoners Cut Wood Near Kane." February 1, 1945.

———. "Letters from Niver Brothers." October 11, 1945.

———. "Veterans, Attention." May 31, 1945.

———. "Walter Taylor Reminisces on Eliot Ness's Last Years." March 22, 1961.

Punxsutawney (PA) News. "Decade Brings Vast Radio Change." January 22, 1930.

Punxsutawney (PA) Spirit. "Brookville Man Comes Thru Japanese Attack on Hawaii." December 17, 1941.

———. "Draft Boards Notified of 112 Critical Occupations." August 22, 1942.

———. "DuBois Uses Curfew as Check to Polio." August 29, 1944.

———. "Formation of a Civil Defense Force in Pennsylvania Is Under Way Today." March 1, 1941.

———. "House Prepares to Pass Vinson Navy Bill as War Clouds Hover in East." January 30, 1934.

———. "No Business Depression Is Feared Despite Stock's Fall." November 7, 1929.

———. "Washington." December 17, 1941.

———. "WPA Victory Gardens Produce Tons of Needed Vegetables." September 19, 1942.

Reiff, Ron. "Pieces of the Past: Sherwood Refining Co." Your Daily Local, December 14, 2022. https://yourdailylocal.com/pieces-of-the-past-sherwood-refining-co.

Research Brief. "Pennsylvania's Oldest Baby Boomers Turn 65." https://pasdc.hbg.psu.edu.sdc/pasdc_files/researchbriefs/BabyBoomer_RB.pdf.

Ridgway (PA) Record. "Anne Marie Hargrave." https://www.legacy.com/us/obituaries/ridgwayrecord/name/anne-hargrave-obituary?id=13483356.

Sacramento (CA) Bee. Obituary for Wilbur Joseph Jackson, January 23, 2000.

Seiler, Eddie, Sol Marcus and Bennie Benjamin. "When the Lights Go On Again." Recorded by Vaughn Monroe and His Orchestra. Released in 1942.

Shamokin (PA) News-Dispatch. "Shamokin Group Tours U.S. Plant." July 14, 1943.

Stanford. "Full Committee Hearing on Statement Made by Gen. James A. VanFleet, 1953." https://searchworks.stanford.edu/view/11019008.

State College News. "Gangsters to Grandmothers: Prohibition in Central Pennsylvania." https://www.statecollege.com/articles/local-news/gangsters-to-grandmothers-prohibition-in-central-pa/#google_vignette.

Stevens, S.K., State Historian. "Pennsylvania's First Year in World War II." *Pennsylvania's History* 10, no. 2 (April 1943). Penn State Libraries Open Publishing. https://journals/psu/edu/phj/article/view/21421.

Sunbury (PA) Daily Item. "Counselor to Assist Valley Plant Women." June 10, 1942.

———. "POW Guards Win Army 'E.'" January 8, 1944.

Sykesville (PA) Post-Dispatch. "Nurses Are Needed for Service with the Army and Navy." August 14, 1942.

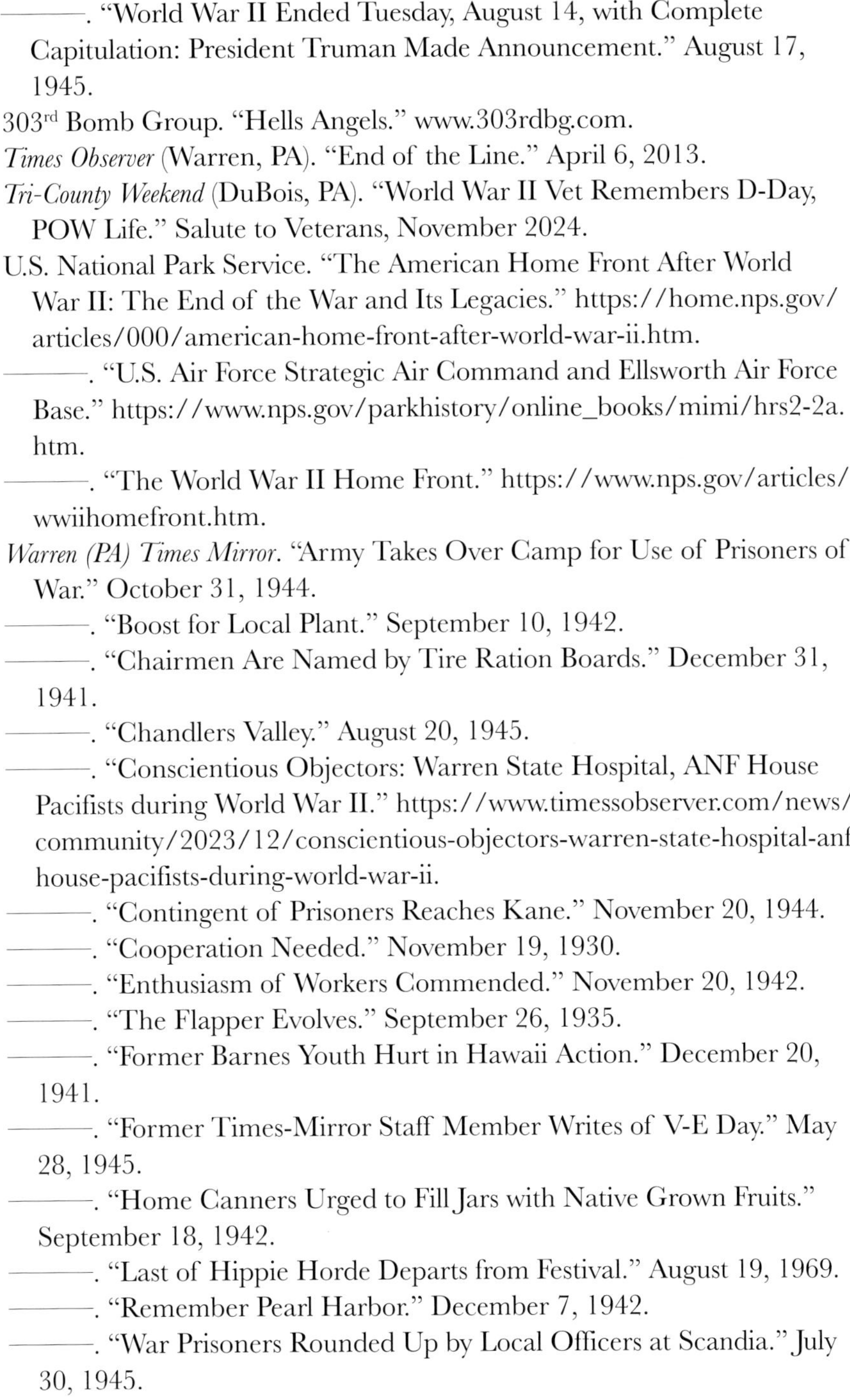

———. "World War II Ended Tuesday, August 14, with Complete Capitulation: President Truman Made Announcement." August 17, 1945.

303rd Bomb Group. "Hells Angels." www.303rdbg.com.

Times Observer (Warren, PA). "End of the Line." April 6, 2013.

Tri-County Weekend (DuBois, PA). "World War II Vet Remembers D-Day, POW Life." Salute to Veterans, November 2024.

U.S. National Park Service. "The American Home Front After World War II: The End of the War and Its Legacies." https://home.nps.gov/articles/000/american-home-front-after-world-war-ii.htm.

———. "U.S. Air Force Strategic Air Command and Ellsworth Air Force Base." https://www.nps.gov/parkhistory/online_books/mimi/hrs2-2a.htm.

———. "The World War II Home Front." https://www.nps.gov/articles/wwiihomefront.htm.

Warren (PA) Times Mirror. "Army Takes Over Camp for Use of Prisoners of War." October 31, 1944.

———. "Boost for Local Plant." September 10, 1942.

———. "Chairmen Are Named by Tire Ration Boards." December 31, 1941.

———. "Chandlers Valley." August 20, 1945.

———. "Conscientious Objectors: Warren State Hospital, ANF House Pacifists during World War II." https://www.timessobserver.com/news/community/2023/12/conscientious-objectors-warren-state-hospital-anf-house-pacifists-during-world-war-ii.

———. "Contingent of Prisoners Reaches Kane." November 20, 1944.

———. "Cooperation Needed." November 19, 1930.

———. "Enthusiasm of Workers Commended." November 20, 1942.

———. "The Flapper Evolves." September 26, 1935.

———. "Former Barnes Youth Hurt in Hawaii Action." December 20, 1941.

———. "Former Times-Mirror Staff Member Writes of V-E Day." May 28, 1945.

———. "Home Canners Urged to Fill Jars with Native Grown Fruits." September 18, 1942.

———. "Last of Hippie Horde Departs from Festival." August 19, 1969.

———. "Remember Pearl Harbor." December 7, 1942.

———. "War Prisoners Rounded Up by Local Officers at Scandia." July 30, 1945.

"War, WWII/Misc (b&w) 1941–1945." Photographic vertical files, Events (01179). Eberly Family Special Collections Library, Penn State University Libraries.

Wellsboro Gazette Combined with Mansfield Advertiser (Wellsboro, PA). "Blackout All Night Tonight." June 24, 1942.

———. "An Explanation." August 11, 1943.

Wellsboro (PA) Agitator. "New Ordway Housing Development to Hold Open House in Elkland, 27th, 28th." October 25, 1956.

———. "Tire Rationing in Effect Soon." December 31, 1941.

Wessman, Alice L. "A History of Elk County, Pennsylvania, 1981." Elk County Historical Society, 1981.

Williamsport (PA) Sun-Gazette. "Francis Kennedy: They Had to Invent Their Own Equipment." November 17, 2018.

———. "Lieut. Litherland Missing Over France." March 18, 1944.

———. "South Williamsport WWII Casualty Identified; to Be Buried in Lycoming County." May 23. 2023.

———. "War Bride Among Group Admitted to Citizenship." May 7, 1947.

"Windcrest, b&w. undated." Photographic vertical files, Physical Plant (01184). Eberly Family Special Collections Library, Penn State University Libraries.

WNEP. "World War II Pilot Shares Stores at Piper Cub Fly-In." https://www.wnep.com/article/news/local/clinton-county/world-war-ii-pilot-shares-stories-at-piper-cub-fly-in/523-19c05c41-6923-8098-763e12fde5df.

Zippo. "Our History." https:www.zippo.com/pages/about-us.

ABOUT THE AUTHOR

Kathy Myers is a native of Ridgway, Elk County, Pennsylvania, where she spent most of her life. She was the director of marketing at Elk County General Hospital in Ridgway, and prior to her retirement, she was the owner of Area Abstracting and Filing Service, a real estate settlement/title abstract company serving attorneys in Clearfield and Jefferson Counties. A member of the seventh generation of her family to live in the Wilds, Myers is a historian, genealogist and writer who now resides in the Beechwoods of Jefferson County. She is a member of the General Society of Mayflower Descendants (GSMD) and is the founder and past governor of the Winslow Heritage Society. She has published pieces in local newspapers and in the *Mayflower Quarterly*, an international publication, and she has contributed to the *Watershed Journal*, a local literary publication.

Myers served her community as president of the Ridgway Area School Board, as president of the Elk County General Hospital Auxiliary and as president of the Elk County Recreation and Tourist Council. She served on the GSMD 2014 Congress Planning Committee, researched and compiled *Junior Mayflower Descendants* booklets for the GSMD Juniors Program, was a chairperson of the GSMD Marketing Committee and served as membership chair and assistant to the historian for the Society of Mayflower Descendants in Pennsylvania. She was regent of the DuBois-Susquehanna chapter of the Daughters of the American Revolution. Myers is a juried member of the Wilds Cooperative of Pennsylvania.

Myers is the author of *Historic Tales of the Pennsylvania Wilds*, *The Pennsylvania Wilds and the Civil War* and *A History of Benezette: Heart of the Pennsylvania Wilds*, all published through Arcadia Publishing/The History Press.

She is married to her high school sweetheart, John, and they are the parents of one son and have two grandsons.